Lynching Barack Obama

A Psychological-Political Analysis of the White Man's Addiction to Power

Dr. Tobias E. LaGrone

Copyright © 2014 Dr. Tobias E. LaGrone

All rights reserved.

ISBN: **1503375668**
ISBN-13: **978-1503375666**

DEDICATION

This book is dedicated to the black men of the earth, and to all men of every race, ethnicity and nationality, who believe in the human dignity and worth of all God's people. This book is dedicated to the freedom fighters from every nation and tribe, who dares to speak truth to power and demand that justice roll down like waters and righteousness like a mighty stream. This book is dedicated to those black men of courage, who broke the chains of slavery, bore the burden of segregation, and under extremely harsh conditions made the difficult decision to become who they could, so that future generations might become who they were born to be.

(Revision 4)

CONTENTS

1	Why Power Addicted White Men Hate Barack Obama	1
2	Defining Power Addicted	23
3	Political Lynching of Barack Obama	38
4	Confused Psyche; Selective Amnesia of White America	92
5	Punish the Majority for Voting for Obama	103
6	Newt Gingrich Says Obama Thinks Like A Kenyan	111
7	In Your Face: Arizona Republican Governor Jan Brewer Treats Obama Like a Little Black Boy	115
8	Voter Suppression and American Apartheid	118
9	Barack Obama; The Right Kind of Black that Some White People Can Accept	130
10	How the Election of the First African-American President Benefited the White Power Elite	132
11	Obama's Mistakes	145
12	2014 Midterm Elections: Republican Strategy to Remind Red State Whites to Hate Barack Obama	173

BOOK'S DESCRIPTION

President Barack Obama has encountered resistance from Republican Tea Party politicians since his first day in office. The first African-American President has been the target of racist attacks and political sabotage like no other President in recent history. This book uses psychological-political analysis to interpret the irrational behaviors of Republican Tea Party politicians and the people they represent. This book examines the psychology of race, prejudice and the power addicted behaviors of white males in positions of power and privilege.

ACKNOWLEDGMENTS

Thanks to the historical black colleges and universities of Rust College, Holly Springs, MS, and Jackson State University, Jackson, MS; thank you for nurturing my love of learning and prompting my intellectual awakening. Thanks to the generations of church members of New Prospect Missionary Baptist Church, Nettleton, MS, and Poplar Springs C.M.E. Church, Shannon, MS; thanks for nurturing my soul and teaching me the truth of God's Word and teaching me about my worth as a person who is unconditionally loved by the God of the universe.

CHAPTER ONE

WHY POWER ADDICTED WHITE MEN HATE BARACK OBAMA

While growing up in rural Mississippi I never thought that I would see the day when an African-American man would be sworn into office as President of the United States of America. I contend that it is God's providential hand that made this possible. Barack Obama is the right man for our times. He is highly intelligent, overly patient, politically savvy, and strategically calculating; God used President Obama to help pull the world back from the cliff of a financial abyss that was created by the false promises of trickle-down economics, Wild West deregulatory policies of Ronald Reagan's disciples and weak willed Democrats who threw America's poor under the bus of capitalistic greed.

Let there be no mistake about the intent of this book, I am writing this book from the perspective of an African-American male who knows racism and bigotry when I hear it, see it and feel it. I am writing this book in order to inform Black people and other oppressed people of the world that; No, you are not imagining this! No, your mind is not playing tricks on you! Racism is real, and those power addicted white males who are in power relish in making you feel like you are imagining it. The power addicted gets some type of deviant psychological reward when they see Black people and other minorities get frustrated with a racist system of white privilege that plots for our failure. I am convinced that the sabotage we see happening to President Obama is the same type of sabotage that Black Males have endured for hundreds of years in America.

You may ask, why use such direct racial language like; white men, power addicted white males, and white thought process? I use such direct racial language because this is what is called for at this juncture in our historical analysis of world systems, a world system that has been shaped by white male thought processes. The power addicted white male thought pattern does not recognize other races and ethnicities as being equal in human worth and value, and therefore, this white male skewed thought pattern has intentionally shaped the world's economic, political, legal and educational systems to disproportionally benefit the white men of the world.

While being reared by my parents and grand-parents in the Deep South State of Mississippi, I was taught that my life could literally hinge on my ability to 'read' what a white person was thinking. If my innocent childish behaviors were mistaken by some white person as being some type of act of disrespect towards them, then what happen to Emmett Till could possibly happen to me.

I have over 40 years of experience analyzing, dissecting the thought processes, thinking patterns, and psychological rationales of the white male psyche. I grew up in a family where I had the privilege of being influenced by my maternal great-grandfather, Rev. Jean Fields, who was born a slave and was raised by slave parents. I have been educated by those with first hand knowledge about the behaviors and thought patterns of the power addicted white males.

In order for our world to begin to heal from the trauma of economic, political, and judicial exploitation that a power addicted white male agenda has inflicted upon this world, we must drag the ugly demon of racism and white supremacy psychological complex out from the dark crevices of secrecy into the shining light of God's truth.

The disrespectful treatment that America's first African-American President is experiencing originates from the racial psyche of the power addicted white male. What the power addicted white male is discovering is what many African-Americans have known for decades, that the world has people from all shades and hues who are great thinkers and leaders, and the power addicted white man's vision is not the only vision that is suited for shaping and directing the world we now live in.

President Obama has been treated like a fugitive vandal and an American villain; the right wing has questioned his origin of birth, called him a socialist, compared him to Hitler and even accused President Obama of trying to destroy the country, when the sad reality is that everything they have accused President Obama of; the facts of all these accusations point to President George W. Bush, but being that they see President Obama as 'less than', less than a white male, then he must be the problem. I am convinced that those who are behind this media campaign to discredit President

Obama know the truth to some degree, yet they like throwing red meat to those gullible poor white people who will take the bait and contribute money to Republican Tea Party causes.

These poor white people don't have the intellectual willingness to understand that they are being used as puppets to advocate for a system that keeps them poor as well. All they really have to cling to is the idea that; "At least I am not black." For some of them, identifying with the Republican Party gives them some sense of self-worth. Somehow they feel so close to their oppressor that they are willing to endure some of the same abuses and exploitations that many minorities experience just to get the psychological reward of hearing the oppressor say, "Good job in helping us keep the Black Folks, Mexicans and Latinos in their place, we are all on the same team!" The reality is that the oppressor who holds the wealth lives a life that is far different from the poor white person he uses as a pawn in his game of oppression. The Koch brothers have stored up wealth for 50 generations of their descendents, while the poor white man and woman that are used as their pawn cannot even afford to send their own child to community college.

Since the election of President Obama, there has been an increase in the number of American hate groups and the membership of state militias, both groups consist of primarily white men. The power addicted white male is experiencing a form of mental psychosis, whereas he can not believe that America is changing demographically. Census data tells us that by the year 2048 minorities will outnumber America's white population. The thought of this demographic shift is frightening to the power addicted white male because he can not fathom being viewed as a minority. In the mindset of the power addicted white male, to be a minority means that you are 'less than' and the power addicted white male can not psychologically handle the thought of being considered as 'less than'.

The power addicted white male is born into a world of white power and white privilege; his self-esteem is boosted when he hears that Columbus discovered America, that all the founding fathers of this country were white men, and for the most part, he has only had to answer to other white men; whether he was at the bank, in the classroom, on the job, on the football field, at the court house, in the military, etc., the white male has only answered to the white male. This is the reason why many black public schools were integrated into white schools during the desegregation period; after integration, those black leaders who had been principals at the all black segregated public schools were forced to take a lesser position of a classroom teacher or assistant principal under the direction of the white male principal. State legislators could not fathom the idea of giving all black schools equal funding on par with their white counterparts, so the lesser of the two evils in the eyes of the power addicted while male was to close the black public schools and integrate them with the white schools under the careful supervision of the white master/principal. Some black high schools were demoted to being the integrated primary or elementary school. This gave the perception to the African-American community that the all black high school which once was the pride of the African-American community, was now 'less than' good enough when compared to the white high school that black children would be bused to.

Another racially motivated factor for demoting African-American school administrators was the fact that white parents did not want their white children under the authority of a black school principal or teacher. White parents refused to allow their children to be disciplined and/or paddled by a black person because of the belief that a black person should never be in a position of authority over a white person.

According to the National Center for Education Statistics (NCES), the majority of students in public schools across the United States will be non-white for the first time in American history. NCES estimates that 49.8 percent of all American students this coming school year will be non-Hispanic white students. At just under 50 percent, white students will still be the biggest racial group represented in US schools, but they will no longer make up the majority of all students in the country. According to the Associated Press, the NCES projects that nearly 25 percent of minority students will be Hispanic, while 15 percent will be black and another five percent Asian. Biracial and Native American students will make up the rest of the minority stake in schools.

The power addicted white male is fearful that African-Americans and other minority groups will unite and do to the power addicted white male what he has done to minorities. The power addicted white male can not psychologically process what it means to feel helpless; he is frightened to see Black people in positions of authority and power. It is un-nerving for the neo-patriotic white male to have to salute an African-American Commander and Chief. These are issues of the psyche and soul that the power addicted white male must face and process in a healthy psychological and spiritual way.

America is changing rapidly; the genie is out of the bottle and there is no going back. Instead of the power addicted white male seeking out common ground with minority groups for a more just and equal society, he is conspiring to enact voter suppression schemes and judicial rulings that seek to keep the Negro and other people of color in our 'place'. The power addicted white male has some type of psychological impediment, whereas he doesn't like to share anything; he is a hoarder, a hoarder of money, a hoarder of resources, a hoarder of power and privilege. The power addicted white male doesn't want a society where the Kingdom of God becomes manifest; a society where we are not divided by social caste, race, or socio-economic status.

Tea Party Believers act as if Black people are not human beings and in many ways today some people continue to believe the slave masters' propaganda that Black people are somehow subhuman. We are talked about in the media as being welfare dependent, food stamp cravers, and hand out pleaders, when the political pundits and media owners know for a fact that poor white people are the largest recipients of American welfare benefits. I call these white welfare recipients the 'Wal-Mart Poor'! They work at Wal-Mart and like me, mostly shop at Wal-Mart, they are the working poor, yet they are too proud to join forces with minorities and fight for economic justice and a living wage. They are so proud of being white until they make themselves content to be economically poor, but racially 'privileged'.

The psychological political games that white males have played with African-Americans can be described as sociopathic behaviors; think about how white male corporate leaders and their board of directors uses the profits of capitalistic gain to fund political candidates that will make laws that favor low wages, long work hours, minimum employment security, and little recourse for workers who have been abused and/or wrongfully terminated. These same corporate and political leaders then use verbiage that tell African-Americans and other poor people that we are solely to blame for our lack of social and economic success. These corporate and political leaders are either delusional or just plain purposefully attempting to inflict psychological torment upon those who are most vulnerable in society. I really think that they get a thrill out of watching the have nots struggle, scratch, and claw trying to make it in this fixed socio-political economic game. As a therapist I have discovered that when ever someone continues to engage in a deviate behavior that either hurts their self, others, or both, then there is some type of emotional reward and pay off that the perpetrator is receiving and enjoying at the expense of others, and even at the expense of one's own long term self-interest.

Some white men who are in positions of power act as if we are not human beings because we are black. I have watched how the professional athletic organizations of the National Football League and National Basketball Association have created rules that govern and suppress mostly African-American athletes who naturally and spontaneously desire to celebrate their accomplishments on the court or the field. Football players in both the college and professional ranks will be given a penalty if they celebrate or show any type of emotion after scoring a touchdown or scoring a pivotal basket. Black males are being emotionally sterilized because these professional leagues know that some white people who are watching these sporting events can not stand to see a black man express his power and athletic prowess in a dominating way, especially if his abilities can not be adequately duplicated by a white counterpart. Football players will be penalized if they take off of their helmet on the field of play after making a great play, they tell us that this is in the best interest of player safety; however, another more covert reason is that some white men don't want to look at the face of the black player. The NFL wants the dominating black male to be masked and covered by the color of the team uniform and helmet, while the white athlete is made to be the 'face' of the franchise. It is strange how mostly white professional hockey players can fight and engage in brutal violence, and they are applauded, but if a black athlete in the ranks of professional sports expresses these same type of actions then he is characterized as dumb brute, an evil beast, and a thoughtless savage. No, I am not promoting violence of any kind; I am just pointing out some facts!

We can witness how a referee can make a terrible call and the black athlete's natural emotion is expressed and the black athlete is penalized for this expression and for pleading for justice to be served. The commentators focus on the emotional outburst and expression that the black athlete makes and barely acknowledges that the referee made a poor call that resulted in a natural human response from the athlete. For the most part, this is what Black males have been asked to do when dealing with the white oppressor, we have been asked to take it on the chin, suffer in silence, grin and bear it and maybe we will get benevolent 'make up' call somewhere down the road.

Why am I as a black male being asked to be emotionally sterile when it is my emotions that make me who I am? My emotions fuel my rhythmic genius! Why am I being asked to act as if I am 'soul-less' just in order for some white people to feel comfortable around me? Why is it that you love my emotions and my passion when I am dancing like Michael Jackson, signing like Aretha Franklin, or playing like John Coltrane, but when I begin to cry out for racial equality, social justice, and a level playing field, then I am no longer a welcomed guest in this American house?

I have concluded that my emotions are not the problem, my rhythm for life and soulful expressions are not the problem; the problem lies in the white males' soul-less behaviors of oppression and exploitation. The white male is fearful of showing his emotions and having compassion for people who don't look like him; he is fearful of being called a nigger lover and a bleeding-heart liberal. He is afraid of being kicked out of the pack of white male privilege, exiled from the herd and left outside of the privileged class to fend for himself. The white male's lack of emotional self-awareness continues to lead him into acting out his own unprocessed sub-conscious frustrations on other races that he must see as less human in order to justify his brutal inhumane acts. As long as the white male can keep his race looking for an enemy that is 'other than' white, then he can avoid looking into the mirror and coming to grips with the pain, misery, and human cost that hundreds of years of slavery, colonialism, capitalism and selfish greed has wreaked upon the human race.

Power addicted white male, I will not believe your lies, which attempt to make me believe that I am some type of sub-human monster. No, I will not accept it! I did not unleash the atomic bomb upon the world. I did not impose the electric chair, gas chamber and the lynching noose upon our society. I did not institute Jim Crow laws, and mass incarceration driven by unjust racial policies. I did not sanction the Tuskegee Experiments and the eugenics of forced sterilization upon our most vulnerable citizens. I did not transport millions of Africans from their native land, rape their women, dehumanize their men, mute their language and work them as human property for hundreds of years. I did not extinguish the Native American and then claim their land as my own. No! I am not the monster!

It is no accident that some white agitators attempt to insult Michelle Obama by calling her a monkey or ape. It is no accident of language when some shout 'Obama go back to the jungle'. This language is learned language passed down from one generation to the next. They are believers in the lie that Africans are sub-human, these people operate in ignorance, being denied the truth that the continent of Africa is the mother of all civilizations, and our Black ancestors are the fathers of intelligent behavior, culturally astute civilizations, medical advances, and advanced systems of reading, writing, architecture, and engineering. The White man believes that he is superior to the rest of God's creation. When he shouts U.S.A.; he feels that the rest of the world should bow in humble obedience to kiss the feet of the white master.

The power addicted white male even found a way to exploit the tragedy of September 11th, by branding the number 9-1-1 (September 11th, 2001) as a blank check and manipulative marketing tool to wage war on anyone who disagrees with the Neo-cons of the Bush Administration. September 11th, provided these war hawks with the perfect opportunity to manipulate the reptilian brain of the collective unconscious of the white masses in order to wage an endless war of terror against any one who disagrees with the white male ideology of how the world should be shaped and governed. The term 'terrorist' became a 'catch-all phrase' for every world government who wanted to label any oppositional voices that may challenge the exploitive model of corporate greed, capitalistic oppression, or the tyranny of a dictatorship. Capitalism and democracy become even more synonymous, meaning that if you question any part of the capitalistic model then you must be a socialist, an insurgent, a terrorist. No intellectual debate every took place in the public sphere that raised the question; Why would a human being be so desperate to be heard or to exact revenge that one would become a suicide bomber? What grievance does this person have? Are any of those grievances legitimate articles for discussion and global debate?

The power addicted white male specializes at labeling people as something other than 'human', other than 'normal', something other than being worthy of being heard and treated as a human being. The power addicted white male likes to minimize the voices and human worth of any one who does not think and act like he does, because he doesn't want to engage in the hard work of intellectual debate and cognitive processing that will encourage him to take a hard long look at his internal self and ask the question; "What have we done, as white men, to cause so many people in the world to hate us?"

CHAPTER TWO
DEFINING POWER ADDICTED

What is addiction?

According to the National Institute on Drug Abuse; <u>The Science of Addiction: Drugs, Brains, and Behavior</u>, addiction is defined as a chronic, relapsing brain disease that is characterized by compulsive drug seeking and use, despite harmful consequences. It is considered a brain disease because drugs change the brain—they change its structure and how it works. These brain changes can be long lasting, and can lead to the harmful behaviors seen in people who abuse drugs. I am suggesting that the emotional feeling that one experiences when residing in a position of power, when one is exercising power 'over' others, and when one feels entitled to reside in positions of power while feeling others are not worthy of such power positions, are all controlled by neuro-chemical responses in the human brain whereas the brain's neuro-transmitters provides the power addicted person with a reward response that reinforces power addicted behaviors. This is much like most drugs of abuse which directly or indirectly target the brain's reward system by flooding the circuit with dopamine. Dopamine is a neurotransmitter present in regions of the brain that regulate movement, emotion, cognition, motivation, and feelings of pleasure. The overstimulation of this system, which rewards our natural behaviors, produces the euphoric effects sought by people who abuse drugs and teaches them to repeat the behavior.

The work of German historian and professor, Soenke Neitzel and German historian, professor, and social psychologist Harold Welzer in their book; <u>Soldiers: Diaries of Fighting, Killing and Dying,</u> or <u>Soldaten</u>in the German language, the book is an analysis of the secretly recorded interrogations of 13,000 World War II German Nazi military prisoners who were interrogated by British Intelligence Officers. According to the article written by Allan Hall for Daily Mail U.K., in review of Neitzel and Welzer's book, Allan Hall wrote in the article: <u>The 'perfect, pitiless, Nazi': German soldiers' confessions reveal how troops driven by bloodlust killed innocent civilians for fun;</u>

"Chilling confessions of POWs captured by the British have laid bare the brutality and excesses of 'ordinary' German soldiers in the Second World War. A book of transcripts to be published in Germany next week reveals how the honour of its old army was lost amid the frenzy to be 'perfect, pitiless Nazis'. In the interrogation transcripts, the German soldiers speak of the 'fun' and 'pure enjoyment' of massacring innocent civilians and enemy troops. One Luftwaffe airman, identified as

Pilot B, relates the 'enormous fun' he had in shooting fleeing civilian columns on the packed roads of France and Belgium in 1940. 'When we were in low-altitude flight over the roads, if cars came to meet us, we kept the headlight on, that made the drivers think that there was oncoming traffic. Then we let rip with the cannon. It was a great success, beautiful, enormous, fantastic fun!" he says. In another interview, the same pilot speaks about trying to machine-gun homes in Ashford, Kent, during the Battle of Britain. He said it was 'fabulous' to see windows rattle on the houses. He said: 'As we came around the roofs would fly off. Wow! And on the marketplace we saw people gathered, people talked. We squirted off the guns. That was fun.' Another told of an attack on Eastbourne, saying: 'We did a low level attack. We got there and there was this big house with a ball going on. There were lots of women in evening gowns and a band. We turned round and gave it to them. My dear fellow, that was fun!' Another boasted: 'In our squadron I was known as the "professional sadist". I knocked off everything: buses, a civilian train in Folkestone. I gunned down every cyclist."

As a therapist I have been trained to analyze what is the reward that the patient is receiving from his/her dysfunctional behavior. People engage in behaviors, no matter how absurd and harmful those behaviors may be to one's self or others, because there is some type of psychological-emotional reward that the patient receives. A therapist can not help the patient find resolution to the dysfunctional behavior until we discover what is the 'pay-off' that the patient is receiving from this behavior? When we read history and assess the many stories of Nazi Germany soldiers who committed horrendous atrocities against the Jewish people and other groups they deemed as undesirable, the soldiers tried to pacify their conscious and justify their evil behavior by saying 'I was only following orders'. I think the actions and thought processes of Nazi Germany soldiers need to studied and re-examined very closely today from a socio-psychological perspective because this language sounds very familiar as Black America listens to white male police officers who have shot and killed unarmed Black men in America.

According to the article written by Ryan Gabrielson, Ryann Grochowski Jones, and Eric Sagara for ProPublica entitled; <u>Deadly Force, in Black and White, a ProPublica analysis of killings by police shows outsize risk for young black males</u>; "Young black males in recent years were at a far greater risk of being shot dead by police than their white counterparts – 21 times greater, according to a ProPublica analysis of federally collected data on fatal police shootings. The 1,217 deadly police shootings from 2010 to 2012 captured in the federal data show that blacks, age 15 to 19, were killed at a rate of 31.17 per million, while just 1.47 per million white males in that age range died at the hands of police. One way of appreciating that stark disparity, ProPublica's analysis shows, is to calculate how many more whites over those three years would have had to have been killed for them to have been at equal risk. The number is jarring – 185, more than one per week. ProPublica's risk analysis on young males killed by police certainly seems to support what has been an article of faith in the African American community for decades: Blacks are being killed at disturbing rates when set against the rest of the American population."

In my next book I will cover that matter in far greater detail but I will speak on it some hear as I lay the context for this current book. As a therapist I am asking myself; how could policemen continue to apply extreme pressure to the body of the 43 year old Eric Garner of Staten Island, New York, who was accosted by primarily white policemen for selling loose cigarettes? Daniel Pantaleo is a young Rambo type white male policeman who has had citizens making prior complaints regarding Pantaleo using excessive force. Pantaleo leaped on Eric Garner's back like Mr. Garner was a horse or wild beast and wrestled Mr. Garner to the ground with the help of other officers. The video records Mr. Garner saying at least 10 times that 'I can't breathe' while white male policemen applied pressure to his back and upper torso and while Officer Daniel Pantaleo used an illegal choke hold around Mr. Garner's neck. The medical examiner ruled Eric Garner died from compression of the neck, compressions to the chest and "prone positioning during physical restraint by police. The medical examiner rule Eric Garner's death as a homicide.

In the case of Eric Garner's murder, Michael Brown's murder in Ferguson, Missouri, and so many other black male murders throughout this country, we hear the policeman say the same thing that Nazi Germany soldiers said; "I was just doing my job!" People this is frightening to me and it should be frightening to you as well, there is something eerily familiar here. Why is it that a certain type of white male authority figure is able to suppress his conscious and take black lives with impunity? I will cover this theory in great detail in my next book, but I suggest that the same psychological premises that are at play with the death of Jews by the Nazi soldiers, the death of unarmed black men by police, are also present in the social psychology of power addicted white males when it comes to us analyzing how President Barack Obama has been treated by the power addicted white male.

Defining Power Addicted

I am using the words of Power Addicted White Male as terminology to describe a personality profile. I am not using this term in an effort to lump all white men together in this category. Just as with any personality profile there are certain diagnostic criteria that must be present before one can be diagnosed with a particular psychological disorder, this book describes the personality traits and behavior patterns of those persons who met the diagnostic criteria for being Power Addicted.

Criteria for Power Addicted

Power addiction is a maladaptive pattern of behavior leading to clinically significant impairment or distress as manifested in at least three (or more) of the following occurring at anytime in the same 12 month period:

1. Unreasonable expectation to receive preferential treatment because of one's race, gender, ethnicity, and/or social status.
   - Can be coupled with an unreasonable expectation for those of a different race, gender, ethnicity and/or social status to be treated in a 'less than' manner because they are other than.

2. Quick to cause conflict while asserting one's perceived power and /or authority in lieu of engaging in compromise or rational debate:
   - The office and/or position becomes a mask to hide behind and allow one an excuse not to engage in rational debate nor psychologically process what others may think or feel.
   - The power addicted places one's position and perceived power in higher esteem than the needs of the people one was hired, appointed or elected to serve. The letter of the law is always more important than the unique circumstances of the individual.
   - The power addicted doesn't like to engage in intellectual dialogue because one's 'intellectual reasoning' is totally vested in the position of authority one holds, therefore one

reasons from the perspective of protecting the power position and proving the power position to be correct.

3. Gravitates towards vocational positions that provide one with a sense of 'power identity':
   - Seeks to be in charge of something or somebody while feeling that he/she is best equipped to lead regardless of one's lack of qualifications or experience.
   - Avoids relationships that require one to become more attuned with one's higher psychological and/or spiritual self. Feels highly uncomfortable discussing feelings and showing emotions.
   - Allows one's position of power and privilege to define one's identity.

4. Will manipulate and abuse others in order to save face, must always be perceived as being right; to be shamed or to bear guilt is to be viewed as being weak.

5. Rarely, if ever, apologizes and will save face at the cost of minimizing, shaming and embarrassing others.

6. Feels highly uncomfortable and is very reluctant to own one's mistakes, inadequacies, and failures.

This is especially true for those power addicted white males serving in law enforcement, they like the idea that a citizen has to do what he/she is commanded to do or face the threat of being arrested or worse. The power addicted white male can violate a citizen's constitutional rights and use what I call 'blank check statements' that allows him to literally get away with murder. The law enforcement official can justify harming a law abiding citizen by simply saying;

"I felt threatened"

"I thought I saw a weapon"

"The person was acting erratic"

"They fit the description of a suspect"

When I am at the grocery store and at other public venues it is common to see a high number of power addicted white men who make it a point to wear a tee shirt or some other type of clothing identifying one's self as being a volunteer firefighter, river rescuer, emergency medical tech, anything to identify one's self as being special, being different, being above the common crowd, being different than the every day ordinary person. These are honorable professions, yet the power addicted white male has a tendency to allow his intra-personal identity to be shaped to a fault by the power position he holds.

The power addicted white male is more likely to impersonate an officer of the law and have some type of flashing light on his automobile in order to give him an added sense of self importance. The possession and concealed carrying of a fire arm/gun is very important to the power addicted white because of the euphoric feeling of power that the weapon provides. Any power position that provides the power addicted white male with a badge, local, state or federal government identification as being someone important like a judge, district attorney, commissioner, etc, feeds the power identity.

The power addicted white male lives in a self induced cocoon culture that validates manhood based upon primarily three things; the accruement of material wealth, positions of power over people, and the ability to punish opposition by brute force or by legal or economic punishment.

CHAPTER THREE

POLITICAL LYNCHING OF BARACK OBAMA

Lynching was a tool of psychological intimidation that was used much like that of Roman crucifixions. The lifeless limp body of the unfortunate soul that in some way disturbed white people's world was left to hang in public as a warning sign to both black and white people who would seek to disturb the status quo. Lynching would take place as vicious mobs gathered and served as judge, jury and executioner. The intimidation factor is paramount in the lynching event, not only was it intimidating to those who looked like and empathized with the black man being lynched; it also served as sadistic entertainment for those who composed the white lynch mob. This fact provides us insight into the irrationality of those who engage in racial hatred.

Lynching was not just a middle of the night event where some poor soul was dragged from their home in the late hours of the night, in many cases lynching was an after church Sunday afternoon family event. Think about this, they just heard the 'Word of God' preached and mere hours later they are having a picnic while a black man's neck is noosed and swinging from a tree. In some cases the lynching victim was hanged and then set on fire, burnt alive while the crowd went o-o-h and a-h-h! Visit the website: www. http://withoutsanctuary.org/main.html and click on the photos section.

Senator Mitch McConnell made the following remark in an interview that appeared in the National Journal on Oct. 23, 2010; "The single most important thing we want to achieve is for President Obama to be a one-term president." The number one priority of this Senate leader was not to create jobs for Americans, not to implement banking, finance, and mortgage reforms that would safeguard us from those irresponsible behaviors that bankrupted the country and the world economic system, no this white man's number one objective was to make sure that Barack Obama did not get re-elected. Really! Well, Senator Mitch McConnell wasted his time and America's time because President Obama is a two term President!

I contend that the exercise in futility that the Republican Tea Party is engaging in as they attempt to sabotage America's first African-American President has very little to do with the fact that he is Democrat, but a lot to do with the fact that he is an African-American Male. The 'dominant' white male's thought pattern will not allow him to accept that America is waking up, America citizens of various races and political stripes saw through the smoke screen of John McCain, Sarah Palin, Mitt Romney and Paul Ryan and chose a black male over the traditional white candidate. America spoke, Obama won, democracy prevailed, but the psychologically dominance of the traditional white male conservative mind can not accept the decline of his power. In this case the white male has done to Obama what he has always done to those black males who don't fit in with his self serving agenda. He chooses to obstruct, frustrate, and debilitate the black male's ability to succeed by controlling how much money the black man has access to and by distorting the message that the black man attempts to communicate.

These acts of obstruction and frustration that have been thrown into President Obama's path are acts that the conservative white male enjoys engaging in, because in both conscious and subconscious ways he perceives his violent obstructionist actions as physical blows he is hitting Obama with. These hostile acts of disrespect towards President Obama are lynching behaviors that satisfy the power addicted white male's thirst to inflict violence upon the 'uppity' Negro.

The power addicted white male is acting out his hate towards those others, those other than white; the power addicted white male is angry and indeed 'mad' because the world no longer bows at his feet nor worships at the alter of the White American dream. The technology of the internet and satellite television has exposed the American white male to the truth about the world we live in. These technologies house a library of truth in regards to the African origin of humanity, the truth about how our C.I.A. has toppled democratically elected governments in South America, Middle Eastern African and on the broader African continent. I think that the American White male is in shock to some degree, he can not believe that Columbus really did not discover America, many inventions we use today were invented or improved upon by black inventors, and a Black man got elected President and the world did not suddenly come to a horrific end. The lie of white supremacy is slowly unraveling as his fictitious world is being turned up side down.

The power addicted white male is entering into a mental state of psychological neurosis because the truth about himself and other people of the world is too overwhelming for him. He has been taught his whole life that America is the best country on the planet, however we now know that even though America is a great place to be, there are other countries that have a good quality of life and some of them measure higher on the quality of life scale than America does. Middle class suburban white moms are finding out that their children are not the best and brightest that the world has to offer, we are discovering that international test scores are showing that American students are lagging behind several less developed countries in math, reading, and science.

He is not one of us

Growing up in a small southern rural town we immediately knew when someone wasn't from around those parts. We could tell by the way they walked, talked and presented themselves, but it was usually O.K., once we learned that the person was in town visiting a family member, most of the time whom we knew, and many times finding out that the stranger from out of town was a cousin of one of our cousins, our minds became settled that this stranger wasn't a threat to our wellbeing. This is human nature, all of us have preconditioned biases that affect the way we view the world and interact with others, yet our biases gets us into trouble when we allow those biases to cause us to permanently brand people as less than worthy of being treated with human dignity and Godly respect.

The white man in America refuses to acknowledge that he has these preconditioned biases and to a very large degree he allows these preconditioned biases to shape his views about African-Americans and other minority groups. The white man's treatment of President Barack Obama goes far beyond partisan politics, this mistreatment of President Obama has racial overtones that permeate the conversation and behaviors of those Republican Tea Partiers who attempt to undermine President Obama's presidency. President Obama even said; "If I sponsor a bill declaring apple pie American, it might fall victim to partisan politics." The Republicans will vote against anything that Obama proposes! This is the same wall of frustration that most African-American men have faced their whole life; we have been denied jobs, positions of power, business loans, and political office all because we are something other than white. There have been elections through out this country when you had a more intelligent African-American defeated by a less competent white person. As a political scientist I learned early own in campaign strategy that people want to vote for someone that reminds them of themselves.

Let's take a look at some of the events that have grabbed the headlines since President Barack Obama took office, I mean things and events that have never before occurred in the history of the American Presidency; coincidence, I don't think so!

The Secret Service Falls Apart

African-Americas are saying; 'here we go again, a black man becomes President and suddenly the Secret Service is not as good as it use to be'!

The problems with the Secret Service during President Barack Obama's tenure have been numerous. The problems have been so severe until President Obama replaced Secret Service Director Mark Sullivan in March 2013 with Julia Pierson, then Pierson was forced to resign in October 2014 after more mishaps.

Why has the most admired protection agency in history suddenly come apart at the seams when an African-American becomes President? African-Americans find this very strange and alarming!

Here is a chronological listing of the Secret Service troubles since President Barack Obama took office. The timeline is taken from NBC. Com, see this link; http://www.nbcnews.com/news/us-news/long-list-breaches-scandals-secret-service-under-obama-n215751

November 2009: A Washington couple, Tareq and Michaele Salahi, crash Obama's first state dinner. The Secret Service later acknowledges that officers never checked whether they were on the guest list.

A photo emerges showing that they shook hands with the president. Sullivan, the director, says that he is "deeply concerned and embarrassed" by the breach. The Salahis parlay their fame into an undistinguished career in reality TV.

November 2011: A man with a semiautomatic rifle parks in front of the White House and fires at the building, with Sasha Obama inside and Malia Obama on her way home. A Secret Service supervisor, mistaking the shots for car backfire, orders officers to stand down. The service does not figure out that shots hit the building for four days, and only then because a housekeeper noticed broken glass. The president and first lady are infuriated, The Post reports years later.

April 2012: Eight Secret Service agents doing advance work for a presidential trip to a summit in Colombia lose their jobs after allegations that some took prostitutes from a strip club back to their hotel rooms. A Justice Department investigation finds that two Drug Enforcement Administration agents arranged one encounter between a prostitute and a Secret Service officer. Obama later says: "When we travel, we have to observe the highest standards."

May 2013: A Secret Service supervisor leaves a bullet in a woman's room at the Hay-Adams hotel, which overlooks the White House, and allegedly tries to force his way into the room to retrieve it. An investigation finds that the supervisor and a colleague sent sexually suggestive emails to a woman subordinate. The supervisor loses his job, and the colleague is reassigned. A Secret Service spokesman says: "Periodically we have isolated incidents of misconduct, just like every organization does."

March 2014: Three Secret Service agents responsible for protecting Obama in Amsterdam are placed on leave after a night of drinking, in violation of Secret Service rules. One of the agents is passed out drunk in a hallway, The Post reports. The newspaper reports that the three are part of what is known as the counter assault team, a last line of defense responsible for fighting off assailants if the president or his motorcade comes under attack.

Sept. 16, 2014: In perhaps the most chilling of the Secret Service lapses, a security contractor with a gun and an assault record gets on an elevator with the president during a trip to Atlanta. The Post, citing people familiar with the incident, reports that the contractor used his cell phone to take video of Obama and did not stop when Secret Service agents told him to. The Secret Service only learns that the man has a gun when he is fired on the spot and turns it over. Obama was not told, The Post reports.

Sept. 19, 2014: An Iraq war veteran with a knife jumps the White House fence, dashes through the North Portico doors and makes it deep inside the building, into the East Room, before he is tackled, and only then by an off-duty Secret Service agent. The Secret Service first says only that the man was apprehended after getting in the door. A congressman tells The Post that a security alarm was disabled because staff nearby found it too noisy.

Speaker of the House Rejects President Obama's Request

Speaker of the House, Congressman John Boehner wrote a letter to President Obama on August 31st, 2011, rejecting the President Obama's request to address a joint session of Congress on

Wednesday, Sept. 7, 2011, instead Boehner proposed that President Obama address the joint session of congress on Thursday, Sept. 8, 2011. This is the first time in American history that an American President has been denied such a request. Some will say what is the big deal, but when you begin to add up all of 'the firsts' that has happened to President Obama, then one must look for the common denominating factor that could help to explain why America's first African-American President is being treated time and time again in such a grossly disrespectful manner.

The truth of the matter is that the Republican Tea-Party leaning base loves this type of stuff, they love to see that Obama Negro put into his place by the 'strong white' male leader. John Boehner was merely tossing red meat to his good ol' boy crowd. These acts of disrespect by John Boehner, other Republicans and Tea Party leaders are acts that mimic the power addicted white male's anthem of 'stand your ground'. To hell with America creating more jobs, forget about education reforms, failing schools, and our crumbling American infrastructure, the power addicted white male would rather see it all fall to the ground before he allows Barack Obama to get credit for anything that strengthens the American economy. The power addicted white males in Congress are dead set on sabotaging President Obama's efforts to help the average working class person, the power addicted white male is fine with the economy being the way it is because whether the economy booms or busts, he is going to be fine regardless. The salary of a United States Congressman or United States Senator is $174,000 dollars per annum, so whether he passes a bill or not, he still gets paid.

Do Nothing Congress

According to a Washington Post article written by Opinion Writer, Dana Milbank, July 1st, 2014; "Congress has passed just 56 public laws this year, for a total of 121 since the beginning of 2013. This virtually guarantees the current Congress will be the least productive in history, well behind the "do nothing" Congress of 1948, which passed more than 900 bills." Republican Tea Party obstructionists are dead set on frustrating President Obama's progressive agenda of modern immigration reform, increased educational funding for low incomes students and prospective students, and raising the minimum wage to a livable wage. The Republican Tea Party obstructionists are standing their ground and their Red State constituents are blindly applauding the ignorance of this type of governance strategy. The economically poor white people in Red States are allowing their deep rooted anti-African-American, anti-immigration reform views to cause them to support politicians and policies that works against their own self interest.

Throw More Road Blocks in Obama's Way

As of March 2014, Republican Tea Party Congressmen have voted 54 times to repeal the Affordable Health Care Act, which they have maliciously named Obama Care. This behavior can be viewed as an Obsessive Compulsive Disorder. When polls are taken, some of the same poor white people who are in favor of the Affordable Health Care Act, say that they are against Obama Care, their racial hatred of President Obama blinds them to the fact that the Affordable Health Care Act and Obama Care are literally one in the same. Those power addicted white males who manipulate the public, especially poor white voters, know exactly what they are doing; they are engaging in psychological warfare that is aimed at keeping the working masses divided. The interest of working poor African-Americans and working poor White Americans are the same, both groups want deceit housing, good paying jobs, low crime communities, affordable healthcare, affordable quality education for themselves and their children, and the hope that the next generation will do just a little bit better than the previous one. Think Tanks and political pundits manipulate the facts, distort the truth and use differing religious views to keep our nation divided, all the while helping the rich to get richer.

In an article written by Steve Benen for MSBNC.com, <u>Falling Like Dominos, Red-state Governors expanding Obama care</u>; "As of a week ago, about half of the nation's states had embraced Medicaid expansion through the Affordable Care Act, while the other half seemed to be motivated almost entirely out of partisan spite. But in recent days, there's been a burst of unexpected activity on this issue. Pennsylvania Gov. Tom Corbett (R) struck a deal with the Obama administration that will allow Medicaid expansion to cover another half-million low-income Americans in the Keystone State. A day later, Tennessee Gov. Bill Haslam (R) said he expects to follow suit in the coming weeks. Ruby-red Wyoming generally resists any voluntary federal program, but it, too, is starting to come around on Medicaid expansion. Indiana Gov. Mike Pence (R), a fierce "Obamacare" critic, recently did the same."

In this same article Steve Benen reports how racial disdain and partisan spite towards President Obama serves as the primary factor as to why a Utah State Representative, who is also a medical doctor, stated that Utah citizens having access to medical care 'could cause harm'. Well, we are all aware of the possibility of medical error, but really, you are so desperate to spite President Obama and tow the Republican Tea Party line until you, a medical doctor who swore an oath to do no harm, would actually say that people are better off without access to any health care rather than for them to benefit from affordable health care backed by President Barack Obama. I plead with all intelligent, Christ loving people, to open your eyes and see how ludicrous this 'anti-anything Obama' pathological behavior is. The Republican Tea Party group has become the party of no; no to anything that does not fit the power addicted white male's agenda of controlling the masses and keeping them subservient to the ruling rich class, and no to anything that looks like it will offer validation to the Presidency of Barack Obama.

The Stand Your Ground Mentality of the Power Addicted White Male

The Stand Your Ground Laws that have been instituted throughout the United States of America is another indicator of the power addicted white male's unwillingness to engage other human beings in a cordial and intelligent manner. The power addicted white male thirsts for war and not peace, because his psychological world view only makes sense to him when he views the world through a war lens. It is us, the white man, against the rest of the world. If you are an American then you must bow down and assimilate to our white way of doing things, this is what the power addicted white man believes. He believes in assimilation, an American melting pot where every race and ethnicity is dumped into the melting pot and comes out thinking and behaving like the prototypical power addicted white male. The political history of this country is rooted in White Male Power Pathology, whereas the white male feels that he has inherit authority and 'right' to exercise his will as he pleases. The American Indian was not respected as a human being; the power addicted white male from Europe systematically exterminated a whole race of people and claimed their land as his own. The power addicted white male operated with an air of racial superiority, carrying the idea that he had the 'divine right' to take the Americas as his own. Everywhere the White European male has gone he has left a trail of death and destruction along with ethnic and cultural degeneration.

At the heart of his inhumane behavior towards other races and ethnic groups is the belief that he is racially superior to other people. I contend that the core psychological drive within the psyche of the power addicted white male is the belief that he is 'better' suited to be in charge and in control. For over 200 years, since the founding of this country, the American white male has been taught by his predecessors that white men are beyond reproach and that a minority can not stand on equal footing with a white man. For hundreds of years the white male has lived comfortably in positions of power, privilege and prestige knowing that public policy, economic policy, media commercials, real estate, automobiles, sports leagues, religious institutions were being designed to cater to his wants, needs, and desires. For hundreds of years the white male has been the number one marketing demographic therefore businesses tailored there advertisements to appeal to him. As we approach the year of 2020, the white male is being forced to read the writing on the wall, white men and white people will soon be in the minority in America. The power addicted white male is experiencing psychological neurosis as he sees media outlets catering to demographics who are African-American, Hispanic, Latino, and Asian. He is in shock that an African-American male got elected President of the United States. He is having extreme difficulty adjusting to the changing complexion of America.

The stand your ground laws, conceal and carry laws, and open carry gun laws that are highly valued by white males have become more and more popular.

According to criminal.findlaw.com, the Stand Your Ground Law is explained in this manner; "It is impossible to discuss stand your ground laws without first explaining the concept of the duty to retreat. In its most extreme form, the duty to retreat states that a person who is under an imminent threat of personal harm must retreat from the threat as much as possible before responding with force in self-defense. These days, states that retain the duty generally incorporate a variety of the duty with somewhat less stringent requirements. Stand your ground laws are essentially a revocation of the duty to retreat.

Stand your ground laws generally state that, under certain circumstances, individuals can use force to defend themselves without first attempting to retreat from the danger. The purpose behind these laws is to remove any confusion about when individuals can defend themselves and to eliminate prosecutions of people who legitimately used self-defense even though they had not attempted to retreat from the threat. In many states with stand your ground laws, a claim of self-defense under a stand your ground law offers immunity from prosecution rather than an affirmative defense. This means that, rather than presenting a self-defense argument at an assault trial, for example, an individual could claim self-defense under the state's stand your ground law and avoid trial altogether.

States with Stand Your Ground laws differ on whether the law applies to instances involving lethal force, with some states retaining the duty to retreat when lethal force is involved and others removing the duty to retreat under all circumstances. Controversy over Stand Your Ground laws are often criticized as encouraging violence. Critics claim that the laws lead to a "shoot first, ask questions later" attitude that results in more injuries and deaths than would occur without the law. Proponents of stand your ground counter that the laws allow people to protect themselves without worrying about whether they have retreated sufficiently before using force." (See more at: http://criminal.findlaw.com/criminal-law-basics/stand-your-ground-laws.html#sthash.3iwJrZYz.dpuf)

Stand your ground laws are designed to make the power addicted white male feel safe and secure. These laws are reminiscent of how black people use to have to cross to the other side of the street when they saw white people coming. A black man would have to bow his head and not look a white man in the eyes because to look a white man directly in the eyes was considered threatening and disrespectful to the superior white male. Stand your ground laws were designed to provide the power addicted white male with the power to 'kill at will' if he at anytime perceives himself to be in danger. This is a strange and troubling law, as a therapist I understand that a person's perception is their reality. A person can perceive another person to be a threat when the other person is actually not threatening at all. The predisposed bias of the power addicted white male causes him to view all non-whites as an imminent threat, the power addicted white male is particularly suspicious of the African-American males. It is no accident that the stories that have topped the headlines in the last two years that involved stand your ground laws have consisted of a paranoid white male shooting and killing an unarmed black male.

When I hear people say that 'we want to take America back', I am hearing the rattling of Confederate sabers, I am hearing shouts of 'The South Shall Rise Again'. Those who want to take America back are living in a condition of delusional thinking; they remember a period of time when a black man had no right of which a white man was bound to respect. They remember a time when a white man's word outweighed the credibility of any Black man's word, by mere racial status. They talk about the good old days when everybody lived by the Bible and neighbors looked out for each other. Those good old days were not such good days for my share cropping ancestors and my parents who struggled to get an education in under funded Negro only schools. Those so called good old days were the days of the night riding Klan and lynch mobs that hunted black men for sport; they were not good old days for African-Americans.

Donald Trump Doesn't Like Barack Obama

Do you remember Donald Trump and other conservative political pundits stirring the rumor mill saying that Barack Obama was not born in America? The thought process of rich white men is that Barack Obama is nothing, a nobody, and how dare you attempt to come out of nowhere and ascend to the height of American political power. Donald Trump was born into a wealthy family, his father Fred Trump was a real estate mogul in New York and he left Donald an inheritance in the range of $40 million to $200 million dollars. OK, help me with this, your daddy was filthy rich and left you at least $40 million dollars to start you life with, yet you say that you are a self made man. The white male mind tells it self what it wants to be true, then attempts to rewrite history to fit the fictional narrative that it wants to be true.

After the media and white power brokers turned over every stone researching Barack Obama; you know they searched for mistresses, criminal records, illegitimate children, embarrassing photos, crooked financial dealings, etc., and at the end of the day all they could come up with is that 'he really wasn't born here'.

Barack Obama was born in Hawaii and he has a birth certificate to prove it. The white male mind can not grasp the fact that Barack Obama is intelligent, articulate and capable of leading this country. It is far easier for them to accept George W. Bush, as an in-articulate blue-blood aristocrat that passed himself off as a good ol' boy from Texas, than for them to accept that Barack Obama is the authentic capable person that he presents himself to be.

Let's look at this paradox, George W. Bush faked his self identity, he faked his own personal being by pretending to be just the average Joe, good ol' country boy from Texas. A country boy with degrees from Yale and Harvard that comes from the aristocratic lineage of his grandfather, Senator Prescott Bush and his father, President George H.W. Bush. How does this make George W. Bush an average Joe? Once again the white mind makes itself believes what it wants to believe when it comes to making things fit its myopic view of the world.

Obama! You Lie!

Yes this actually happened, for the first time in modern history a United States Congressman called the President of the United States 'a liar' while he was addressing a joint session of congress. On September 9th, 2009, President Obama stated that health care reform would not cover illegal immigrants and Congressman Joe Wilson, Republican from South Carolina, need I say more; Republican, South Carolina, shouted; "You Lie"! Wilson apologized soon afterwards and was publically rebuked by the U.S. House of Representatives.

Some people were shocked that Joe Wilson would have the audacity to do such a thing, but Black folks were not surprised, we were disappointed, but not surprised. Black people know that the White Man feels like he is a god, an ultimate authority in all things. We were not surprised that Joe Wilson was filled with enough hatred and vitriol towards President Obama, a black man whom people like Joe Wilson feel is beneath him, that he would be audacious enough to call the leader of the free world a lie during such a sacrosanct occasion.

Was Joe Wilson responding to what the President said about illegal immigrants not being covered by healthcare reform as being a lie, or was Joe Wilson subconsciously saying that everything about you Obama is a lie?

Was Joe Wilson verbally expressing his suppressed subconscious thoughts and the thoughts of those like him and what they really feel is this; "Obama you are a fraud and your very existence is a lie? You can't be real, we see it but we don't believe it, a black man is the most powerful man on the planet. This can't be happening because my daddy told me that black people were not smart enough to serve as President of the United States. My world doesn't make since anymore. Obama you are a lie, you are not real, you are a figment of my imagination, I am having a really bad dream, a nightmare!"

Placing all humor aside I am suggesting that Joe Wilson's mind set and others like him may be experiencing some type of racial psychosis, think about it; everything that white men have been taught about black people being ignorant, unable to manage their own lives, etc., has been proven to be a lie, not just by the election of Barack Obama, but by the contributions that African-Americans are making in every part of American life. The last 20 years has seen a rise of young black educated professionals who are teachers, school principals, university professors, medical doctors, attorneys, banking executives, etc., and for the average good old boy this is too much to bare, because in times past when a good old white boy failed to do something productive with his life, he at least had the assurance that he would never fall lower than a black person. He was told that black people are the social and economic floor beneath which no white person will sink.

What else was Joe Wilson thinking? Could it be that he was thinking this: 'How could this be happening, a black man is actually the President of the United States? You can't be smarter than me, you can't be in a position higher than I am in! I am a white man and I have been told that black folks are inferior, lazy, shiftless and here I am sitting in a congressional gathering listening to a funny named Negro named Barack Hussein Obama address me, the nation and the free world as President of the United States of America!'

This type of psychological shock has literally pushed some power addicted white males into a state of mental psychosis where they are engaging in irrational political actions that work against their own self interest.

Tea Party Persona is a mask for White Supremacy

It is no coincidence that America's first African American President was elected in 2008 and the Tea Party became more aggressive and vocal in 2009. The Tea Party is a classic example of how rich white men are masters at manipulating poor unlearned white people into advocating for policies that will benefit wealthy white men and harm poor white people and minorities. The Tea Party didn't just spring up spontaneously as some would like for us to believe. They say that it is a grassroots movement that came about due to the average 'White American' being feed up with big government spending, high taxes and welfare spending. Well the facts point to a very different picture of the forming of the Tea Party.

In 2002 the first website for the Tea Party was launched by the organization, Citizens for a Sound Economy (CSE), this group was founded in 1984 by the ultra conservative Koch Brothers, David and Charles Koch, and received over $5.3 million from big tobacco companies, mainly Philip Morris, between 1991 and 2004. As of today the Citizens for a Sound Economy group has spun off into two other groups, Freedom Works and Americans for Prosperity, they are still funded by the billionaire Koch brothers and other white males who are dead set on making sure that the White male maintains his position of economic advantage and privilege in America and the world. They lobby congress to insure that wages are kept low and the economic climate remains in a place that benefit rich white men. Poor white people like those who work at Wal-Mart and other low wage jobs will campaign for Tea-Party candidates even though they, the working poor, are living in poverty, have no health care coverage and have no means of sending their own children to college. They are delusional to think that their economic well being will be improved by supporting policies and laws that benefit millionaires and billionaires.

White Men in positions of wealth and power promote an invisible caste system that depends heavily upon those poor whites at the bottom rung believing that they can rise to the top. The 'joke' is that in a caste system you will most likely die in the same caste you were born into, as well as your children and grandchildren. It seems that the poor white person at the bottom rung insures that they carry out the agenda of the Big Boss in hopes of being invited up the ladder. Tea Party supporters are against every social program that provides tools for the poor and working poor to climb up the social ladder without being invited by the White Master. One of the reasons why they are in shock of Barack Obama is because they are still trying to literally figure out where he came from. How did he get into and graduate from the Ivy League Schools of Columbia and Harvard? How did he arrive on the scene and none of us from the good ol' boy system anointed him nor gave him access into the world of the political elite and wealthy. Even Hillary Clinton became a little flustered by Barack Obama's rise. They are afraid that more people like him will use education, hard work, and ingenuity to climb the social and political ladder and present a legitimate challenge to the good ol' boy status quo system. What they don't understand is that if God be for you, God is more than the world against you.

The Tea Party is built on a system of manipulation and fear mongering; the Tea Party provides Republicans an 'acceptable place' to show their racial hatred and bigotry towards 'the others', those other than white; mainly towards Blacks, Hispanics, Latinos. The Tea Party provides a place for frustrated White Republicans to openly display their racial prejudices, self serving biases and yearnings to maintain the system of white privilege while hiding behind a Tea Party mask. Some of the political rally signs that have been displayed by Tea Partiers are unashamedly racially motivated.

- Obama-nomics: Monkey See, Monkey Spend!

- Congress = Slave Owner Taxpayer = Niggar

- Obama, the Long Legged Mack Daddy

- What's the difference between the Cleveland Zoo and the White House? The zoo has an African (picture of a lion) and the White House has a lying African.

- Bury Obama with Kennedy (sign reading this is on the ground with horse manure on it).

- Barack Obama supports abortion, sodomy, socialism and the new world order.

- Commander and Chief, Ha!! How about Commandeer and thief!

- Obama is the pirate commander and chief!

- The tree of liberty must be refreshed from time to time, Pennsylvanians are armed and ready.

- I work hard so Obama voters don't have to.

- The American tax payers are the Jews for Obama's ovens.

- Cap congress and trade Obama back to Kenya.

- Obama half-breed Muslin (they mis-spelled Muslim)

- Road sign in front of a business: Obama gives us hopes, dreams and maybe a new holiday. That's my Nigger.

Now I understand how a person can be frustrated that the economy is lagging, America is nearly bankrupt and the world economic system has been shaken, yet what is hard to process is why these angry white people don't blame George W. Bush and Dick Chaney for our country's current social and economic condition? They conveniently refuse to recall that George W. Bush and the Republican neo-cons created this economic disaster in the first place.

As a child I was told that we would never have an African-American President, but if this nation did elect an Africa-American, white folks will have so damaged and wrecked the social and economic structure to such a degree until the first Black President would spend his/her tenure trying to clean up the white's folks mess. White folks would dig the hole so deep until it would take two presidential terms to undo the damage that was done. Sure enough here we are over 40 years later and what I told as a child has proven to be true.

Chronic pattern of racial hatred towards President Obama and His Family

From day one President Obama and his family have been the targets of unwarranted scrutiny from power addicted white males, Republican Tea Party supporters and even some liberal leaning white Democrats can not escape the prejudices of their implicit racial biases. No other

President has been scrutinized and villainized in the same manner that President Barack Obama has been. Let's take a look at the chronic dysfunctional behavioral patterns that some power addicted whites have engaged in while verbally assaulting the President of the United States of America.

- Then Senate Majority Leader Harry Reid, a Democrat, described Obama as a light-skinned African-American with no Negro dialect unless he wants to use one.

- Former Governor of Illinois, Rod Blagojevich stated to the Enquire Magazine that; "I'm blacker than Barack Obama. I shined shoes. I grew up in a five-room apartment. My father had a little laundromat in a black community not far from where we lived. I saw it all growing up." (Here we see a power addicted white male Democrat who equates shining shoes with being Black.)

- Minnesota State Senator Mike Parry sent out tweets on his Tweeter account stating; "Barack Obama is a power hungry arrogant black man". (This type of language is reminiscent of power addicted white males describing a well educated and astute Black Person as being 'an uppity Negro.)

- President Bill Clinton when referring to Obama, while trying to curry the support of Senator Ted Kennedy for then Presidential hopeful, Hillary Clinton; Bill Clinton was heard saying; "A few years ago this guy (Obama) would have been getting our coffee."

- Kansas Representative Lynn Jenkins stated; "the GOP (Republican Party) is searching for a "great white hope" to stop President Obama's policy agenda." (This type of language is reminiscent of how the white community would await a white male hero to come and save white folks from the salvage black male beast.)

- Dr. David McKalip, the then president-elect of the Pinellas County Medical Association, a Florida neurosurgeon and opponent of President Obama's healthcare reform initiative, sent out an e-mail containing an image of President Obama as an African witch doctor, dressed in a loin cloth with a bone through his nose. The caption underneath the picture was the words "Obama Care: Coming Soon to a Clinic Near You."

- The former Fox Television talk show host, Glenn Beck weighed in on President's Obama's decision to make a statement regarding renowned Harvard Professor Henry Louis Gates being arrested at his own home by a white police officer for suspicion of being a burglar. Glenn Beck accused President Obama of being a racist who has a deep seated hatred for white people and the culture of white people.

- The California newspaper, Merced Sun-Star reports that they obtained seven e-mails that Atwater, California, Councilman Frago sent from October 2008 to February 2009 from an anonymous source. "Some compared Obama to O.J. Simpson while others suggested that "nigger rigs" should now be called "presidential solutions." Perhaps the most overboard e-mail was sent on Jan. 15, 2009. It read: "Breaking News Playboy just offered Sarah Palin $1 million to pose nude in the January issue. Michelle Obama got the same offer from National Geographic."

Frago admitted sending the e-mails, but showed no regret. "If they're from me, then I sent them," he said. "I have no disrespect for the president or anybody, they weren't meant in any bad way or harm." The list of people who either sent or received the e-mails reads like a who's who of Atwater community and political leadership, including a county supervisor, a former police chief, a city manager, a former city council member, a former president of a veterans group, a former grand knight of the Knights of Columbus, among others."

- Logan Smith writing for South Carolina television station WIS News 10 reported that in June of 2009; "A state Republican activist has admitted to and apologized for calling a gorilla that escaped from the Riverbanks Zoo Friday an "ancestor" of First Lady Michelle Obama. A screen capture of the comment, made on the Internet site Facebook, was obtained by FITS News, the website of South Carolina politico Will Folks. The image shows a post by an aide to state Attorney General Henry McMaster describing Friday morning's gorilla escape at Columbia's Riverbanks Zoo. Longtime SCGOP activist and former state Senate candidate Rusty

DePass responded with the comment, "I'm sure it's just one of Michelle's ancestors - probably harmless." DePass told WIS News 10 he was talking about First Lady Michelle Obama. DePass has been involved in state politics for decades, and helped elect Republican Governor Jim Edwards in 1974. He was an early South Carolina supporter of former President George W. Bush in 2000."

- Tennessee State Republican Staffer, Sherri Goforth, a legislative aid for Republican state Sen. Diane Black, was reprimanded in June 2009 for forwarding an e-mail image showing all the pictures of previous American Presidents, but when it came to President Barack Obama Sherri GoForth showed him as having only a set of HUGE WHITE EYES on an all BLACK CANVAS.

- Republican activist Mike Green, was caught by the Indigo Journal tweeting, "I just heard Obama was going to impose a 40% tax on aspirin because it's white and it works."

- Sean Delonas, a cartoonist for the New York Post created a controversy when his cartoon appeared in the New York Post showing two white police officers, one with a smoking gun, standing over a dead chimpanzee with the words, "They'll have to find someone else to write the next stimulus bill." (This was around the same time that President Obama had signed the federal stimulus bill into law).

- In 2008, Chaffey Community Republican Women group put out a newsletter in October 2008 with an image of "Obama Bucks", these "Obama Bucks" were made like food stamps with Obama's head placed on a donkey with pictures of fried chicken, watermelon and ribs floating around President's Obama's head.

- Former Florida Republican Leader and former chairman of the Hillsborough County Republican Party, forwarded an e-mail in October 2008 written by Republican volunteer Ron Whitley that stated; "I see carloads of black Obama supporters coming from the inner city to cast their votes for

Obama. This is their chance to get a black president and they seem to care little that he is at minimum, socialist, and probably Marxist in his core beliefs. After all, he is black — no experience or accomplishments — but he is black."

- Virginia Republican Leader Bobby May, when he was the treasurer of the Buchanan County Republican Party, wrote a column for the Virginia Voice shortly before Obama's election questioning whether Obama would change the American flag to include the Islamic symbol or divert more aid to Africa so "the Obama family there can skim enough to allow them to free their goats and live the American Dream."

- Kentucky Representative Geoff Davis stated at a Republican sponsored dinner when referring to Barack Obama; "I'm going to tell you something: That boy's finger does not need to be on the button. He could not make a decision in that simulation that related to a nuclear threat to this country."

- California Republican Politician, Marilyn Davenport's emails depicts President Obama as a chimpanzee being held by his chimpanzee parents. Superimposed on the digitally altered image was the caption; Now you know why he has no birth certificate!

- During the 2012 Presidential election campaign, Billionaire casino magnate Sheldon Adelson donated $10 million to Mitt Romney's Super PAC, and announced publically that he was willing to spend $100 million dollars or more to ensure President Obama is not re-elected. Ok! Filthy rich ultra conservative white man who makes his money off of the vices of the working poor, uses the working poor's money to support anti-working poor Presidential candidate Mitt Romney. Adelson is by far the biggest political donor in American politics. Before this latest contribution, he had given more than $26 million to Super PACs in 2012, according to the Center for Responsive Politics. That includes the $21.5 million he gave to Newt Gingrich's Super PAC, which single-handedly kept the former House Speaker's presidential campaign alive.

- Wisconsin Republican Congressman, Rep. Jim Sensenbrenner criticized Michelle Obama's body shape while attacking her national "Let's Move" healthy eating campaign. Sensenbrenner was overheard talking on the phone, retelling an incident maligning Michelle Obama: "She lectures us on eating right while she has a large posterior herself."

- Donald Trump offered to donate five million dollars to the charity of President Obama's choice if the President would release his academic records, birth certificate, passport and other personal information. Trump continues to lead the insane birthers' charge to convince people that President Obama is not an American citizen.

Andrew Adler, publisher of the Atlanta based Jewish Times, devoted it's January 13th, 2012 newspaper edition to discussing Israel's problems with Iran. Adler laid out three options and option number three was for Israel to order its American based Mossad agents to assassinate President Barack Obama.

Adler stated; "Three, give the go-ahead for U.S.-based Mossad agents to take out a president deemed unfriendly to Israel in order for the current vice president to take his place, and forcefully dictate that the United States' policy which includes its helping the Jewish state obliterate its enemies. Yes, you read "three" correctly. Order a hit on a president in order to preserve Israel's existence. Think about it. If I have thought of this Tom Clancy-type scenario, don't you think that this almost unfathomable idea has been discussed in Israel's most inner circles? Another way of putting "three" in perspective goes something like this: How far would you go to save a nation comprised of seven million lives...Jews, Christians and Arabs alike? You have got to believe, like I do, that all options are on the table."

You read this correctly, Adler is advocating for

the assassination of President Obama in order for Vice-President Joe Biden to take Obama's place.

I suggest that if the publisher of an African-American newspaper had said something remotely similar about President George W. Bush, the owner and staff of the newspaper would have been branded as terrorists and shipped to Guantanamo by the end of that same day.

Last but not least, Republican Party staffer Elizabeth Lauten criticized the Obama's teen age daughters who were acting like typical American teenagers who would be bored to tears at a 'turkey pardoning ceremony' at the White House. Elizabeth Lauten wrote; "Dear Sasha and Malia, I get you're both in those awful teen years, but you're a part of the First Family, try showing a little class. At least respect the part you play. Then again your mother and father don't respect their positions very much, or the nation for that matter, so I'm guessing you're coming up a little short in the 'good role model' department. Nevertheless, stretch yourself. Rise to the occasion. Act like being in the White House matters to you. Dress like you deserve respect, not a spot at a bar. And certainly don't make faces during televised public events."

WOW! The really ironic things about Lauten making such a statement is that she was arrested at age 17 for misdemeanor larceny after she allegedly stole from a Belk Department store in North Carolina, according to court records. The charges were dismissed since Lauten was a first-time offender and she didn't get into additional trouble.

CHAPTER FOUR

CONFUSED PSYCHE; THE SELECTIVE AMNESIA OF WHITE AMERICA

For weeks leading up to the 2010 mid-term election media outlets heralded the inevitable defeat of most democratic candidates and true to prediction many Republican and Tea Party candidates were successful in their bid for public office. The question I dare to raise is this; "How could White Americans be so impatient with President Obama's efforts to repair the broken economy he inherited from George W. Bush?"

The only way I can rationalize the irrationality of these white, working poor, and unemployed middle class voters supporting the Republican and Tea Party candidates is to examine their behavior from a socio-psychological perspective. In the field of mental health my colleagues and I use a term called psychopathology to describe the pattern, the origin, development, and manifestations of mental or behavioral disorders.

The abnormal behavior of poor whites and unemployed middle class Americans voting for Tea Party and Republican candidates is, in the words of Rev. Al Sharpton, like a chicken voting for Colonel Sanders of Kentucky Fried Chicken.

White America's abnormal behavior is indicative of someone who is experiencing Post-traumatic Stress Disorder. According to the American Psychological Association, Diagnostic and Statistical Manual of Mental Disorders, 4th Edition, Text Revision, Post Traumatic Stress Disorder (PTSD) is an anxiety disorder resulting from exposure to a traumatic event in which both of the following were present: 1.) The person experienced, witnessed, or was confronted with an event or events that involved actual or threatened death or serious injury, or a threat to the physical integrity of self or others.

2.) The person's response involved intense fear, helplessness, or horror.

All of America in general and those White Americans with white supremacy ideals in particular, have been traumatized over the last decade by three events which psychologically invoked feelings of intense fear, helplessness, horror, and challenged the ingrained belief of American White Supremacy and invincibility! America's Republican leaning Tea Party activists are now dealing with Group Post-Traumatic Stress Disorder. I surmise this based upon the following facts;

First of all, for many of the post baby boom era Americans, September 11th, 2001 was the first major publically visible display of anti-American sentiment from parties hostile to America on

American soil. Until this horrific event many of my generation had heard of terroristic attacks in other countries that were aimed at American interests, but September 11th, 2001, was our up close and personal Pearl Harbor like event. We were forced to deal with the reality that there are other people in the world who have different political, social, economic, and religious views than ours. Suddenly, for us, the American opinion was no longer the only opinion that counted the most in the world.

Secondly, America began to intimately experience the Wal-Mart driven phenomenon of corporate globalization, whereas products are made cheaply in developing countries and shipped to American stores like Wal-Mart and sold at low prices, yet what many high school and minimally skilled factory workers soon found out is that these low priced goods came at a hefty price in the long term. Outsourcing of low skilled jobs and rising

American unemployment was the ultimate disastrous result. With the complete economic meltdown of 2007, suddenly the days were gone when Bill and Sue could finish high school or even drop out of school, go down to the local furniture factory or automobile factory and secure a lifetime job paying on average $20.00 to $30.00 per hour with health benefits and retirement.

To compound the jobs' issue is the fact that there are thousands of men and women who have mortgages, have children in college, and growing families to sustain, yet they find themselves laid-off from a factory job or low skilled service sector job that they have had since they were 18 years old, right out of high school, and suddenly they are 20 years into marriage, paying the mortgage, and putting their children through college and now they find themselves at the age of 38 years old, too young to retire, unemployed with no marketable skill set for the technology oriented job market of today; and even if they do find a job, they are entering the position at entry level pay which is way below the $20.00 -$30.00 per hour pay their lifestyle is budgeted for.

Many people have been forced to down-size their standard of living by moving out of their dream home into smaller homes, forfeiting automobiles, and even moving back in with their parents along with two or three children of their own, and these are the fortunate ones who have family members who are financially able toss them a safety net; not to mentioned the foreclosure crisis and the countless numbers of families effected. What these people have experienced is traumatizing, especially for those whose personal identity, purpose, and meaning was attached to their job and the material goods it provided for them.

Thirdly, with America having hit rock-bottom in terms of our economy, corporate bail-outs, and global anti-American sentiment, even white conservative voters were frustrated with the failed policies of George W. Bush and the neo-con agenda and as a result, Democratic Party nominee, Barack Obama, became a contender for the presidency. The election of President Barack Obama traumatized those mostly white working class males who were reared in a white supremacy culture, whereas they were taught to believe that an African-American could never get elected to the highest office in American politics. President Obama's election, coupled with the fall of the great American Empire's dominant reign on the world stage, has caused the Republican leaning Tea Party segment of our society to become even more traumatized.

It is conclusive among African-Americans that no matter how well President Obama performs in office there are some segments of our society that will not be satisfied until another 'good old boy' white conservative male occupies the Oval Office. The unprocessed traumatized psychological issues of the Republican leaning Tea Party segment is on full display in the vehement hatred and anger that is being expressed towards President Obama. Subconsciously this segment of society realizes that President Obama is not the blame for their misfortunes, yet to be angry at George W. Bush and his failed economic and domestic policies is like being angry at their 'self' because of who and what George W. Bush represents; the good 'old boy system of white power and white privilege ideology. During the days of slavery and Jim Crow segregation the white man was deemed as always being right; no matter how incompetent or misguided his actions may have been when it came to his dealings with people of color. In the collective unconscious of many Americans, this white supremacist ideal stills holds true today, and is the primary reason for the dumping of all of America's problems on the shoulders of President

Obama, with purposeful selective amnesia in regards to George W. Bush's failures, both domestically and internationally.

In addiction counseling, the addict often finds reasons to blame any and everybody for his/her life crashing and burning! In this 'pre-contemplation stage' the addict has no perception of having a problem and sees no need for change, at this juncture the addict is living in denial. The longer the addict and /or mental health patient remains in denial and refuses treatment, the deeper the psychosis becomes and the longer the recovery will take. Parallel to the addict's behavior is that of the White American Tea Party activists who consciously believes that America's problems began with the election of President Barack Obama. The Tea Party Activist is motivated to fight against the Washington establishment "NOW", but when President George W. Bush was in office these same Tea Party activists would label any protesters of President Bush as being unpatriotic and a terrorist sympathizer! Subconsciously the Republican Tea Party activist allows President Obama's African-American race to serve as a point of galvanization to fight Obama under the guise of fighting big government.

President Obama was elected based upon a message of hope, while many anti-Obama candidates are getting elected with a message of hatred. America is entering into dangerous territory with radical white preachers praying for the assassination of the President, Tea Party activists and militia groups calling for armed resistance against 'Obama's Socialism', while others are daring to hold mass rally Koran burnings to spite the same Muslim nations we need as our allies in the legitimate war on terror and ending armed conflict in Iraq and Afghanistan. This type of temperament and social un-ease can lead to disastrous consequences for our nation if the newly elected congress of 2015 doesn't work with 'our' President to create new jobs, reinvigorate hope, and develop a renewed sense of unity within these UNITED States we call America.

CHAPTER FIVE

PUNISH THE MAJORITY FOR VOTING FOR OBAMA

I have suspicions that leading up to the 2012 presidential election, some power addicted white male C.E.O.s who were in a position to hire thousands of people, intentionally refused to hire people because they did not want the economy to get a boost under President Barack Obama's leadership. Big business wanted Obama out of office in order to get Mitt Romney elected. Big business knew that Mitt Romney, a former business executive whose net worth is estimated at around 250 million dollars would allow big business to once again run wild and further exploit the workers of America.

Power addicted white males are very well organized and cohesive in their vision for the world; maintain white male dominance at all cost. The suppressing of the economy by laying people off of work, downsizing, exporting jobs over seas are not only tools to maximize profit while exploiting the poor, these are also tools that are used to dismantle the American middle class. The American middle class has been devastated by the economic meltdown of 2008 and it has been super wealthy power addicted white men who benefited the most from this coordinated financial catastrophe.

The aim has been to suppress economic growth to such a degree until moderate Republicans, Conservative Democrats, and straddle the fence independents will not dare place another inclusive liberal minded personality like Barack Obama in the White House again. The strategy of the power addicted white male is to frustrate the efforts of America's democratic majority. Frustrate, Frustrate, Frustrate, don't let that Negro succeed, at all cost, just don't allow the Negro to succeed! No matter what President Obama does he can not satisfy the power addicted white male. What we see happening to President Barack Obama is the same thing that the power addicted white male has been doing to African-American men throughout the cities and towns of America. The power addicted white banker will deny a small business loan to an African-American and then take the same business model or idea and give it to one of his family members and then provide the loan money to start up the business. The power addicted principal and teacher will be overly zealous in enforcing the rules when it comes African-American students, yet be lenient and very understanding when it comes white students.

These acts of frustration by the power addicted white male, is basically a form of gorilla warfare whereas he is intentionally sabotaging any efforts of social and economic progress that an African-American or other minorities attempt to make. The power addicted white male views punishment as a means of power. This is why he likes to say he is tough on crime, he enforces the law, he believes in the letter of the law, the reason why he is so dogged in regards to the law is because he knows the laws were designed to protect him and his interests while punishing those who do not acquiesce to white male power interests.

Throughout small town America white male business owners do not want to hire African-Americans because of various stereotypes that power addicted white males believe about minorities, secondly power addicted white males don't want minorities around because these power addicted white males find it difficult and uncomfortable to adjust their psychological self in an emotional way in order to be sensitive to racial and cultural differences. The power addicted white male would just rather not have minorities around, rather than learn to engage his psychological self in an emotionally sensitive manner.

There are many reports from African-Americans and other minorities of having been harassed and demeaned on the job by power addicted white males who find it psychological satisfying to exert their authority while demeaning and diminishing the human value and worth of African-Americans, Latinos, and Hispanics.

One of the primary reasons the power addicted white male feels more comfortable employing Hispanics and Latinos and other non-English speaking undocumented immigrants is because this population is extremely vulnerable. They have no status as an American citizen, they have few legal rights and the power addicted white male knows that he can exploit an immigrant in every imaginable way and the immigrant is very unlikely to call the police or report the maltreatment to other authorities because of the fear of being deported.

These behaviors by the power addicted white male; acts of employment discrimination, harassment, denying minorities promotions and positions of corporate management, and the increased use of temporary employment services are all tools used to keep minorities struggling socially and economically. The premise is that if the power addicted white male can keep poor whites and minorities scratching and struggling to survive from day to day, paying bills and trying to make a dollar out of fifteen cents, then they will not have the time, emotional will or energy to engage in civic engagement and demand political change.

The tax cuts for the rich that Republican legislatures are promoting on both the national and state levels are nothing more than mechanisms to insure those working classes Americans don't get their hands of enough money to ease their troubled minds. Keep the working class worried, weary and fighting each other while those in charge continue to bask in their power and privilege. This is not rocket science, these are simple games that the power addicted white male uses to make sure that the average American does not have enough money to challenge the status quo. According to the National Priorities Project, tax cuts for the top five percent costs the American people and U.S. Treasury $11.6 million dollars every hour. In 2011 the top money earners got an average tax break of $66,384 while the bottom 20 percent received a paltry tax break of a mere $107.00. Former Labor Secretary Robert B. Reich stated in an article, <u>Why We Really Shouldn't Keep the Bush Tax Cut for the Wealthy</u>, August 2nd, 2010;

"For many years, most of the gains of economic growth in America have been going to the top – leaving the nation's vast middle class with a shrinking portion of total income. (In the 1970s, the top 1 percent received 8 to 9 percent of total income, but thereafter income concentrated so rapidly that by 2007 the top received 23.5 percent of the total.) The only way most Americans could continue to buy most of what they produced was by borrowing. But now that the debt bubble has burst – as it inevitably would – the underlying problem has reemerged."

The underlying problem that Reich is referring to is the problem of corporate greed, low wages and a political system that is infected with corporate lobby money that tilts the economic playing field in favor of the rich.

CHAPTER SIX

NEWT GINGRINCH SAYS PRESIDENT OBAMA THINKS LIKE A KENYAN

Newt Gingrich, former speaker of the house, attempted to define President Obama as something other than American when he made this statement. In an interview with the National Review Gingrich said; "What if [Obama] is so outside our comprehension, that only if you understand Kenyan, anti-colonial behavior, can you begin to piece together [his actions]... That is the most accurate, predictive model for his behavior. This is a person who is fundamentally out of touch with how the world works, who happened to have played a wonderful con, as a result of which he is now president."

What Gingrich is expressing here ends up as an indictment regarding Gingrinch's own white plantation master colonial mind set. Gingrich is saying that Obama is thinking like an African who wants to break free from the social and economic shackles of a European colonial master. O.K., what is wrong with that I ask? Doesn't every enslaved and exploited person desire to be free? " The white power mind set of Gingrinch is communicating that Obama is insane to think that the world can be any different than the way it is now. Gingrinch is saying the oppressed should be content with the current state of social and economic oppression that exists, because besides, the white man's way of doing things is the best way and the only productive way.

Gingrich goes on to say; "I think he (Obama) worked very hard at being a person who is normal, reasonable, moderate, bipartisan, transparent, accommodating — none of which was true," Gingrich continues. "In the Alinksy tradition, he was being the person he needed to be in order to achieve the position he needed to achieve . . . He was authentically dishonest. Obama is in the great tradition of Edison, Ford, the Wright Brothers, Bill Gates — he saw his opportunity and he took it. I think Obama gets up every morning with a worldview that is fundamentally wrong about reality," Gingrich says. "If you look at the continuous denial of reality, there has got to be a point where someone stands up and says that this is just factually insane."

Here we go again, Gingrich is accusing President Obama of being a Chicago city slicker, a slick Willy, a con artist, an insane black politician that is something other than 'normal' by the white male definition of normal; this is racially laced thought processes and language. Gingrich is saying that Obama should bow to the demands of the Republican Tea Party led congress and go along with their agenda because if he doesn't then they will not allow him to accomplish very much. Gingrich is saying that Obama is a tricky, opportunistic, lazy, shiftless, conniving counterfeit who is not worthy of the office he holds. What we hear from Gingrich is what we hear from other power addicted white men; it doesn't matter how America voted, it doesn't matter that the majority of Americans voted twice to support Obama's vision for America over the traditional white male's power vision of America. None of this matters because I, Newt Gingrich, and other power addicted white males, still knows what is best for you and our country.

CHAPTER SEVEN

IN YOUR FACE: ARIZONA REPUBLICAN GOVERNOR JAN BREWER TREATS PRESIDENT OBAMA LIKE A LITTLE BLACK BOY

On Wednesday, Jan. 25, 2012, in Mesa, Arizona at the Phoenix-Mesa Gateway Airport, Arizona Republican Governor Jan Brewer met President Barack Obama on the airport tarmac. Instead of her greeting the leader of the free world in a cordial and respectful manner, the Arizona Governor uses this moment as an opportunity to show her Red State supporters that she knows how to put this 'little black boy' in his place. Governor Brewer engages President Obama in a heated debate and points her finger directly into the President's face. When she was asked what they were discussing that lead to this heated conversation, she stated; "He was a little disturbed about my book. We could have been talking about a million different things," Brewer told reporters. "Bottom line is that he generally wants to talk about amnesty and I want to talk about securing our border."

Jan Brewer was very calculating in saying that she pointed her finger in President Obama's face because he disagreed with her regarding immigration reform which she discusses in her recently released book entitled; Scorpions for Breakfast. Well it is easy to see that Jan Brewer set up this photo op so she could get a boost in her book sales by those who dislike President Obama.

It seems that the meaner you can be, the more popular you are among Republican supporters; take for instance the title of Jan Brewer's book, <u>Scorpions for Breakfast</u>. Why is it necessary for Republicans to promote this Wild West gun slinging mentality? Look at the do nothing congress we have in place, very little has been done to help the working people of our country. All that the Power addicted has to give us is gestures of finger pointing at the black boy who has the audacity to hope for a better America, an America where people make a livable wage, have access to affordable health care, and affordable higher education. My finger in your face Obama tells you that even though you are the President of the United States, you are still a little 'Black Boy' to me!

CHAPTER EIGHT

VOTER SUPPRESSION AND AMERICAN APARTHEID

The power addicted white male agenda is to maintain total domination and control over all facets of the world power structures, which are banking, government, and judicial systems. Many states have passed oppressive laws that make it harder for Americans who do not agree with the power addicted white male's vision for this country. African-Americans, other minorities, the elderly, students and people with disabilities will find it difficult to exercise their fundamental right to vote because of the intentionally oppressive voter suppression laws. In every case the facts are the same, power addicted white men from the Republican Party pass laws that seek to insure that white men remain in control in the face of a major

American demographic shift. Power addicted white men from the Republican Tea Party are the common denominator in the passing of all of these voter suppression laws.

Now I have said it before, not only are power addicted white men passing laws to assure their dominance, they take pleasure in enacting policies, laws and procedures that intentionally frustrate minorities and others that don't agree with them. Yes, they like to see others frustrated, there is some type of psychological high that the power addicted white male receives, he 'gets off' on watching people being frustrated. He 'gets off' on seeing the oppressed push back in frustration against the harm and hurt he has inflicted upon them. He takes pleasure in actually feeling the push back when he sees mass marches, protests, and outcries; he is psychologically experiencing the push back from the oppressed in a pleasurable way. It is at that point of experiencing the push back of the oppressed that he stands back and gloats as he can now actually see the physical manifestation of his internalized power addicted self-will. He is now rejoicing as he exercises his will upon others. The pain of the oppressed feeds the power identity of the power addicted.

These oppressive voter suppression measures include requiring a government issued photo I.D. to vote and proof of citizenship to register to vote, cutting back on early voting, eliminating Election Day registration and new restrictions on voter registration drives and additional barriers to voting for people with criminal convictions. All of these measures have been strategically designed to target vulnerable areas in the lives of minorities, mainly African-Americans, Hispanics and Latinos.

Listen to this craziness, power addicted white male Texas legislators promoted legislation that will allow those with concealed carry gun permits to use those gun permits as official I.D. to vote with, however Texas college students can no longer us their official college student identification as an official I.D. to vote with.

The political strategy behind these voter suppression efforts is to throw as many obstacles in the way of liberal leaning college voters and minority voters as possible, in an effort to frustrate them and dissuade them from exercising their constitutional right to vote.

One of the psychological basis for the power addicted white male to disenfranchise minorities goes back to the idea that minorities do not have the intelligence to govern themselves. Power addicted whites males feel that colonialism and the colonization of so many countries were justified, because 'those savage' non white people did not know what to do with their country's natural resources anyway. The power addicted white male continues to operate in this same psychological pattern, he feels that he is inherently more suited to be in leadership because of who he feels that he is; first and foremost he is white. This is what 'his world' has told him, this is what his parents have taught him, this is his 'truth' that his history has taught him. He believes the lie that world civilization began with the philosophy of the Greeks. He believes that Columbus really 'discovered' America. The power addicted white male believes all the lies of white supremacy propaganda, therefore he both consciously and subconsciously views any race other than American White or European White as less than; less than human, less than capable of governing their own affairs, less than worthy of the dignity of being treated as an equal with white people.

Economics are used as a way to keep communities segregated; history tells us that regardless of the amount of money a minority made, they were not welcomed in most predominantly white neighborhoods. White flight is when black folks and other undesirable minorities move into a neighborhood, white people move further out into the suburbs. Once in the suburbs the power addicted white male takes measures to keep the undesirables from following him to this new community he is building for himself and those like him. The first step that he takes is to make sure that the cost of housing is so expensive until the 'average minority' can not afford to live in that community. The power addicted white male feels that if a minority has enough money to buy a house in the over priced community, then that minority must be an educated working professional who knows how to acquiesce to the demands of the white male power structure.

Wealth, or the lack thereof, is used as a way to draw a clear line of demarcation between the classes; your access to money determines what schools you attend, what community you can live in and the type of health care services you have access to. Access to money affects one's quality of life. What we are seeing throughout America is a re-segregating of our communities and our public school system; if the poor student can only access schools in the community which their parents' income level determines, then the end result is a community and community school, full of poor people, with all the social and emotional effects that these type of mass traumatized environments produce. The power addicted white male uses his control of money as a way to endorse social and economic apartheid. It is a fact that obtaining a high school diploma, college degree, technical trainings and certifications, and professional degrees are proven ways to escape poverty and gain some degree of economic stability, however, for years the power addicted white male has made every effort to cut public funding for higher education, cut financial aide for students, all while releasing the wolves of private bankers to cannibalize borrowers in the student loan market and real estate market.

According to a January 10th, 2014, consortiumnews.com article entitled, How GOP Gerrymanders Away Democracy; "Amid America's demographic changes, Republicans have exploited every trick they can think of to stave off actual democracy, where every vote is respected and equal. One scheme has been to modernize the old practice of "gerrymandering," as Beverly Bandler explains. In Election 2012, Democrats received 1.4 million more votes for the U.S. House of Representatives, yet Republicans won control of the House by a 234-to-201 margin. Thus, the second-biggest GOP majority in 60 years was not the will of American voters. It was gerrymandered. Or, as Republican strategist Karl Rove has said, "He who controls redistricting can control Congress." Gerrymandering has become the preferred way for Republicans to defy the principle of majority rule – or democracy – in an era in which whites are declining as a percentage of the electorate. In other words, it's a way to reduce the political influence of people of color as well as that of white demographic groups that tend to vote Democratic. "Politicians, especially Republicans facing demographic and ideological changes in the electorate, use redistricting to cling to power," said Sam Wang, co-founder – along with Andrew Ferguson – of the Princeton Election Consortium blog. "It's up to us to take control of the process, slay the gerrymander, and put the people back in charge of what is, after all, our House."

The changing demographics in America are causing the power addicted white male to confront an 'Inconvenient Democracy', out of shear desperation the power addicted white male is grasping for political straws and engaging in trickery in order to maintain social, economic, and political power.

The power addicted white male would rather sink the American ship of democratic government before he allows minorities to sail the ship. The blatant acts of voter suppression efforts that we see throughout the country are direct efforts to cripple the democratic process, whereas it is becoming less advantageous for the power addicted white male to abide by the age old rule that the majority rules. For centuries the white population has influenced self advantageous policies by shear numbers and the democratic ideal that the majority rules, however with the numbers of minorities rising and set to over take the white population in a short period of time, the power addicted white male is making a preemptive strike against American democracy.

The power addicted white male desires for America to institute a form of American apartheid;

this is what the voter suppression laws are about. The power addicted white male does not believe that minorities have the intelligence to govern this country, nor positively influence world affairs. The power addicted white male is frightened of the idea of having African-Americans and other minorities in positions of power and decision making authority.

The power addicted white male sleeps soundly at night knowing that he has connections and influence with the power brokers of his community, he depends on his connections and the benefits of white privilege to give him an inside track on carrying out his agenda and keeping him and his family safely above the penalties of law and certain societal restraints. These are a few of the important offices that are coveted by the power addicted white male on the local level:

Judges

District Attorney

Chancellery Clerk

Circuit Clerk

City Planner

City Manager

Sheriff and Sheriff Deputies

Chief of Police and Policemen/Policewomen

Mayor

Newspaper/Media Owners

Television and Radio Station Owners

Superintendent of Education

Principal

CHAPTER NINE

BARACK OBAMA; THE RIGHT KIND OF BLACK THAT SOME WHITE PEOPLE CAN ACCEPT

There is nothing wrong with having a Negro dialect, because after all I am AFRICAN-American. It is bewildering how some white people who are racially biased point out the fact that black people speak with a hint of African dialect and somehow those white people try to make it seem like something bad; once again trying to make African-Americans feel as if they are less than human, less than whites. In the case of Barack Obama, the liberal power elite seized an opportunity to present to African-Americans a 'black' man who was also presentable and acceptable to main stream white America. Obama supporter and liberal Democratic Senator Harry Reid said in 2008 that then presidential candidate

Barack Obama was a light skinned African-American with no NEGRO dialect unless he wanted to use a Negro dialect. These are the types of psychological games that power elite white people play with African-Americans, they make us feel as if there is something wrong with the average everyday African-American person; something that is tainted, unintelligent, and less than human, but every now and then an anomaly like Barack Obama appears among the Negro race and he fits the bill for mainstream white approval. I contend that there is nothing wrong with being an African-American who talks with the dialect of an AFRICAN-American, just like there is nothing wrong with an IRISH-American who speaks with a hint of Irish ancestry, or an ITALIAN-American who speaks with a hint of Italian ancestry. What we must begin to examine from a racial psychological perspective is why do some white people use themselves and their behaviors as a measuring stick for all behavioral norms?

CHAPTER TEN

HOW THE ELECTION OF THE FIRST AFRICAN-AMERICAN PRESIDENT BENEFITED THE WHITE POWER ELITE

In 2008 London Bridge was burning down, the house of capitalism was on fire and all the world could see through the translucent walls of the failed pyramid economy of capitalism. World economies were collapsing because of corporate greed and the devilish behaviors of Goldman-Sachs, Merrill Lynch, AIG, and hundreds of other investment firms, banks, and hedge fund swindlers who robbed the hard working people of the earth out of trillions of dollars of savings, home equity and retirement funds. The number of foreclosures and loss of home equity wealth is staggering. A report from the Pew Charitable Trust reports; "U.S. households lost on average nearly $5,800 in income due to reduced economic growth during the acute stage of the financial crisis from September 2008 through the end of 2009. Costs to the federal government due to its interventions to mitigate the financial crisis amounted to $2,050, on average, for each U.S. household. Also, the combined peak loss from declining stock and home values totaled nearly $100,000, on average per U.S. household, during the July 2008 to March 2009 period. This analysis highlights the importance of reducing the onset and severity of future financial crises, and the value of market reforms to achieve this goal." Other key findings in the Pew Charitable Trust are;

> **Income** – The financial crisis cost the U.S. an estimated $648 billion due to slower economic growth, as measured by the difference between the Congressional Budget Office (CBO) economic forecast made in September 2008 and the actual performance of the economy from September 2008 through the end of 2009. That equates to an average of approximately $5,800 in lost income for each U.S. household.

Government Response – Federal government spending to mitigate the financial crisis through the Troubled Asset Relief Program (TARP) will result in a net cost to taxpayers of $73 billion according to the CBO. This is approximately $2,050 per U.S. household on average.

Home Values – The U.S. lost $3.4 trillion in real estate wealth from July 2008 to March 2009 according to the Federal Reserve. This is roughly $30,300 per U.S. household. Further, 500,000 additional foreclosures began during the acute phase of the financial crisis than were expected, based on the September 2008 CBO forecast.

Stock Values – The U.S. lost $7.4 trillion in stock wealth from July 2008 to March 2009, according to the Federal Reserve. This is roughly $66,200 on average per U.S. household.

Jobs – 5.5 million more American jobs were lost due to slower economic growth during the financial crisis than what was predicted by the September 2008 CBO forecast.

According to Henry C.K. Liu in his article for the Roosevelt Institute entitled; <u>The Crisis of Wealth Destruction</u>, Liu states; "The financial crisis that first broke out in the US around the summer of 2007 and crested around the autumn of 2008 had destroyed $34.4 trillion of wealth globally by March 2009, when the equity markets hit their lowest points. On October 31, 2007, the total market value of publicly-traded companies around the world reached a high of $63 trillion. A year and four months later, by early March 2009, the value had dropped more than half to $28.6 trillion. The lost wealth, $34.4 trillion, is more than the 2008 annual gross domestic product (GDP) of the US, the European Union and Japan combined. This wealth deficit effect would take at least a decade to replenish even if these advanced economies were to grow at mid single digit rate after inflation and only if no double dip materializes in the markets. At an optimistic compounded annual growth rate of 5%, it would take over 10 years to replenish the lost wealth in the US economy."

When we look at the economic, social and emotional trauma that Americans and other people of the world experienced as a result of the white power elite's 'bad behavior', it is easy to understand that the 'natives' became restless. Yes, the natives, the commoners, the everyday ordinary worker who believed in the free market principles of capitalism whereas if you work hard, play by the rules and don't paint outside of the lines, you will do fine in the capitalistic system. What the 2008 economic collapse exposed was that the white power elite were not playing by the same set of rules that we commoners were told to play by. We discovered that the game was rigged in the favor of the investment firms and the white power elite, whereas mortgage backed securities and other junk investment products placed the investment firms in a win-win situation and ordinary investors in a loose-loose situation. According to the New York Times article; <u>Banks Bundled Bad Debt, Bet Against It and Won</u>, by Gretchen Morgenson and Lousie Story, published: December 23, 2009; "Mr. Egol, a Princeton graduate, had risen to prominence inside the bank by creating mortgage-related securities, named Abacus, that were at first intended to protect Goldman from investment losses if the housing market collapsed. As the market soured, Goldman created even more of these securities, enabling it to pocket huge profits. Goldman's own clients who bought them, however, were less fortunate. Pension funds and insurance companies lost billions of dollars on securities that they believed were solid investments, according to former Goldman employees with direct knowledge of the deals who asked not to be identified because they have confidentiality agreements with the firm.

Goldman was not the only firm that peddled these complex securities — known as synthetic collateralized debt obligations, or C.D.O.'s — and then made financial bets against them, called selling short in Wall Street parlance. Others that created similar securities and then bet they would fail, according to Wall Street traders, include Deutsche Bank and Morgan Stanley."

For the first time in my life time I began to hear my friends, both black and white, both Republican and Democrat, both liberal and conservative begin to question the legitimacy of the capitalistic model. For the first time in my life there was a unifying chorus being sung about how the working man and woman were mere pawns in the rich man's game and something had to change. From the year of 2000 to 2008 we witnessed an emptying of the people's treasury where our country went from hundreds of billions of dollars in surplus, to trillions of dollars in debt, funding senseless and unwinnable wars in Iraq and Afghanistan. We had an incompetent legacy President named George W. Bush, whose nonchalant dismissive attitude about the social, emotional and financial turmoil that average Americans were feeling caused even the staunchest conservative Republican to question their own loyalty to the Republican cause. The American economy was in a free fall and the world's economy was going over the cliff and out of the dark, from behind the curtain, steps a first term United States Senator from Illinois named Barack Hussein Obama. The power elite, Wall Street bankers and other business moguls seized upon the opportunity to turn our attention from questioning the fairness of capitalism to focusing on Barack Obama and 'Change We Can Believe In'! Power elites from ordinarily opposing camps, liberal democratic camps and conservative republican camps, came together to support Barack Obama for president; not only was Barack Obama a graduate of prestigious white elite Ivy league universities, he was the son of an African father and White mother. Barack Obama was not the descendents of African ancestors who were brought to America on slave ships; in the eyes of the white power elite, Barack Obama was not 'radicalized' like those black men with slave ancestry, who were taught to be weary of the 'white man', no Barack Obama was black enough to rally the support of the African-American community, and white enough (having a white mother, being an Ivy League graduate, having a wife who is an Ivy League graduate, being raised by white grandparents) to garner the support of mainstream White America. I agree that Barack Obama is a highly competent President and I feel that he has done a great job during his presidential tenure, given the tough economic and political circumstances he inherited from his predecessor; however, I boldly suggest that the White power elite coalesced around the 'IDEA' and 'IMAGE' of Barack Obama, just as much as they coalesced around the competent man, Barack Obama. In order to turn America's attention and the world's attention away from the disastrous melt down of the capitalistic system, the white power elite promoted Barack Obama as 'CHANGE THAT WE CAN BELIEVE IN' and caused us to be emotionally moved by the 'IDEA' and 'IMAGE' of Barack Obama, which suggested that America is making a great amount of racial and social progress by electing an African-American as President of the United States. Here we are several years after President Obama's election and we still have not seen the type of CHANGE that will make a significant difference in the lives of the poor and working poor. African-Americans, the poor and working poor have not faired much better socially or economically under Obama's presidency as compared to George W. Bush's presidency.

Here we are in 2015 and President Obama only

has two years left in his presidency, he is considered a lame duck president and with the outcome of the 2014 midterm election, Obama is now facing the daunting challenge of trying to govern with Tea Party Republicans being in the elected majority in both the House of Representatives and the Senate. Once again the white power elite used Obama to turn the attention of the masses away from the failings of capitalism and corporate greed and now here we are no better off today than we were before we experienced the white power elite's designed Obama marketing slogan of CHANGE THAT WE CAN BELIEVE IN! Now that the social, emotional and economic trauma of 2008 has been absorbed by the masses and many have forgotten about raging against the machine and the upsetting the status quo, the white power elite have retuned to business as usual; laying off workers, driving up shareholders profits, driving down wages, outsourcing jobs to the cheapest slave market economy that they can find, and leaving the average American citizen believing that they will one day hit the capitalistic lottery by being able to get a decent job and pay off a 30 year mortgage. Damn, is this really the best we can hope for in life?

The white power elite are satisfied with the gap between the haves and have nots being so vast, it doesn't bother them that social harm and emotional ills are being caused by their greed driven policies. Recent Census data suggests that the wealth gap in America has increased during the last decade, 2000-2010. The gap between the rich and poor in America has widened, as well as the gap between African-Americans and Whites, as well as between workers with only a high school degree and those with education beyond high school. Data suggests that the benefits of higher education in America are growing (in 2000, households headed by someone with a bachelor's degree were worth 2.4 times as much as those with only a high school diploma; by 2011 the ratio was 3.4). Racial inequality in wealth is growing too, in 2000, white households had a net worth 10.6 times larger than African-Americans; by 2011 it was 17.5. As a result of these dismal social and economic conditions that are being caused by the white power elite, the renowned historian Tony Judt wrote a book addressing the social and emotional human toll of the financial crisis in his book entitled, <u>Ill Fares the Land</u>, he states; "There has been a collapse in intergenerational mobility: in contrast to their parents and grandparents, children today in the UK as in the US have very little expectation of improving upon the condition into which they were born. The poor stay poor. Economic disadvantage for the overwhelming majority translates into ill health, missed educational opportunity, and—increasingly—the familiar symptoms of depression: alcoholism, obesity, gambling, and minor criminality."

CHAPTER ELEVEN

OBAMA'S MISTAKES

When Barack Obama took the oath of office as President of the United States of America on January 20th, 2009, he entered office with a majority Democratic House of Representative and United States Senate. America was ready and desperate for new, bold and innovative leadership, this would have been the ideal time to push the majority democratic legislative branch to pass universal health care coverage, overhaul the financial systems, regulate banking practices, forgive student loan debts, pass comprehensive immigration legislation and bail out the American home owner with a complete wiping clean of the slate for those who were victimized by the predatory lending schemes of bankers and mortgage brokers. Obama did none of these things because he was so concerned about being viewed as the radical, socialist leaning liberal black male Democrat. Obama became overly passive and very much obsessed with appeasing Wall Street; he played right into the hands of the lurking Republicans who were cowering in the shadows, hiding from the angry American public who hated the very mention of George W. Bush's name. The Republicans were cowering, yet waiting for an ideal time to pounce on this new African-American President who has seemingly reinvigorated the hope of the masses. It is no secret that Senate Leader Mitch McConnell was dead set on making Obama a one term president. The power addicted white male never had good will intentions towards President Obama and his political agenda.

Obama believed that if he approached governance with the analytical astuteness of a constitutional lawyer, using reasoning, intellect and bipartisan appeasement, then the Republicans would be forced to work with him to get bills passed for the American people, well this is where the calculated move of the white power elite's decision to pick someone like Barack Obama to be the first African-American President backfired for Obama, but worked well for the white power elite and power addicted white males. On paper Barack Obama was well qualified to be President of the United States, but he has one very important factor missing from his extensive and impressive resume, Barack Obama doesn't understand the racial psychology of the power addicted white male, especially those power addicted white males who are from the southern states of Mississippi, Alabama, Arkansas, Texas, Kentucky, South Carolina, Georgia, etc. The good ol'boy politicians from these southern states don't give a damn about analytical reasoning, intellect, and Socratic debate, they see that you are black and they are white and therefore you as a black man do not belong in a position of power over them. Yes it is just that plain and simple. I laugh at the political commentators who host talk shows as they seem baffled and stunned as they try to find the common denominator as to why the power addicted white males refuse to work in a bipartisan way with President Obama. The common denominator is that Barack Obama is a black man! To the power addicted white male it doesn't matter how smart and intelligent he is. It doesn't matter what school he went to. Obama is a Negro, a darkie, a black man whom is suppose to be mowing their yards, washing their dishes, tending their livestock, and yes, serving them coffee and tea! Obama fell right into the Republican Tea Party Power Addicted White Male's trap by failing to push his agenda in the first two years of his presidency, now here he is in the last two years of his presidency facing a majority Tea Party Republican House of Representatives and United States Senate and I am predicting that they are going to terrorize

Obama in every way that is legally possible. They will do what Obama should have done; use the leverage of having a majority advantage in the house and senate to push the agenda of those who voted them into office. Obama's failure to forcefully push the agenda of the poor, working poor, and the minorities who placed him into office caused these constituency groups to become disappointed, lethargic and apathetic towards believing that change can actually take place, they did not vote in the 2014 midterm elections and as a result, the 2014 midterm elections delivered massive victories for the Republican Tea Party candidates. The manipulative and shrewd political strategies of the Republican Party have literally made Barack Obama and the Democratic Party look like 'Jack Asses'.

Republican strategists made 2014 Democratic mid-term candidates run from President Obama's record of success, yes the

Democratic mid-term candidates ran for their lives away from President Barack Obama. I know it sounds irrational, but we are dealing with an irrational Tea Party Republican and Blue Dog Democrat voter base whose racially influenced psychological defense mechanisms will not allow them to see the successes of President Obama's administration. President Obama stated at his speech at North Western University, October 2nd, 2014; "As Americans, we can and should be proud of the progress that our country has made over these past six years. And here are the facts -- because sometimes the noise clutters and I think confuses the nature of the reality out there. Here are the facts: When I took office, businesses were laying off 800,000 Americans a month. Today, our businesses are hiring 200,000 Americans a month. The unemployment rate has come down from a high of 10 percent in 2009, to 6.1 percent today. Over the past four and a half years, our businesses have created 10 million new jobs; this is the longest uninterrupted stretch of private sector job creation in our history. Think about that. And you don't have to applaud at -- because I'm going to be giving you a lot of good statistics. Right now, there are more job openings than at any time since 2001. All told, the United States has put more people back to work than Europe, Japan, and every other advanced economy combined. I want you to think about that. We have put more people back to work, here in America, than Europe, Japan, and every other advanced economy combined."

How does one argue with the facts of Obama's accomplishments, yet the one common platform that the average 2014 mid-term Republican Tea Party Candidate ran on was that they were going to Washington, D.C., to fight Barack Obama. Race is the driving factor regarding the amount of hate, vitriol and irrational voting behaviors of many Red State voters. When I say irrational voting behavior, let me point out this one fact, the Red States of Arkansas, Nebraska, and South Dakota voted to increase the minimum wage in their states, however they elected Republican candidates that will go to Washington and work with big business to drive down wages and resist any federal efforts to raise the minimum wage. The racial hatred of these Tea Party voters is causing them to be blind regarding their own self interest. Race, race, and race is the primary factor and common denominator that makes sense of the nonsensical behaviors of our political landscape. The issue of Barack Obama's race was such a factor in the 2014 mid-term election until DEMOCRATIC Kentucky Senate Candidate Alison Lundergan Grimes was even afraid to announce publically who she voted for in the 2012 presidential election. Listen to the nonsensical element of this argument, Grimes is on the Democratic ticket for U.S. Senate and she feels that even mentioning the name Barack Obama is detrimental to her chances of getting elected. Well Grimes lost the election anyway because she fell right into the hands of Republican strategists; when she ran away from the black man Obama, she also ran away from Obama's record of economic successes.

Obama's mistake of approving Shirley Sherrod's Firing

President Obama has made the mistake of avoiding the issue of race and prejudice in America; he has not confronted the issue head on. President Obama has attempted to delicately dance around the issue of race and prejudice and only address this most important issue when he is pressed by social and political circumstances to do so. President Obama made a lightweight statement regarding the tragic deaths of Trayvon Martin and Eric Garner, he also held a 'beer summit' at the White House when the notable African-American,

Harvard Professor, Henry Louis Gates was arrested at his own house by a white male police officer under the suspicion of being a burglar. Avoiding the discussion of race is like having a pimple on your nose, everybody sees it, you know it is there, everyone who looks at you knows it is there, but both you and onlookers feel uncomfortable discussing the pimple in the presence of each other but just as soon as you part company the discussion is all about the huge pimple that is on your nose.

President Obama's silence on matters of race reinforces America's willingness to turn a blind eye to this issue. The power addicted white male is accustomed to living in a society that caters to his needs and feelings, in American society it is alright to offend every racial and ethnic group, but don't dare say anything that will offend the white male. When the white male becomes offended by something, he makes it his mission to destroy the one who dared say something that casts a disparaging light on the white male. Power addicted white males have supported Rush Limbaugh, Glenn Beck, and Bill O'Reilly because they degrade, denigrate and verbally lynch black people and other non-white people on a daily basis. Power addicted white males listen to the media broadcasts of men like these because they enjoy having their ignorant biases concerning minorities reinforced. Once again, President Obama doesn't want to be viewed as the angry black male who whines about racial issues but as a result of his passive behavior he is giving every American President who follows him plausible deniability when it comes to addressing the issue of racial prejudice; if Obama, an African-American male did not address the issue then why should I? This will most likely be the response of future American Presidents!

President Obama understands that if a minority

is perceived as making a comment that challenges the white male supportive status quo then they are attacked and pushed off of the national scene into obscurity. The case of Shirley Sherrod is a prime example of how power addicted white males take pleasure in distorting the facts in order to punish someone who challenges the good old boy system. Shirley Sherrod, an African-American female, was forced to resign as a state rural development director for USDA in 2010 after conservative activist Andrew Breitbart posted maliciously edited video clips from a speech Sherrod gave earlier in the year at an NAACP event. The videos appeared to suggest that Sherrod was a racist when in reality the unedited version of the recording showed Sherrod sharing with the audience how she has resisted being racist and malicious to white farmers because her father had been discriminated against in the past. Within a matter of hours, Agriculture Secretary Tom Vilsack dismissed her, acting in consultation with the White House. As time passed the fuller context of Sherrod's remarks emerged, the Obama administration then offered Sherrod her job back, which she declined. In 2011, Sherrod sued Andrew Breitbart and his employee Larry O'Connor for defamation. Breitbart died unexpectedly in 2012, but his wife was substituted as a defendant in the suit.

Obama's mistake of not addressing the rage of white male privilege when Gabrielle Gifford was shot

President Obama missed an ideal opportunity to address the issue of race, prejudice and radicalized Tea-Party terroristic propaganda after the tragic shooting of U.S. Congresswoman Gabrielle Gifford on January 8th, 2011 in Casas Adobes, Arizona. Jared Lee Loughner, who at the time was a 22 year old young white male who was frustrated with the United States government and expressed anti-government views that are very muck like the anti-government views of conservative talk show commentators. In 2010 the flames of the divisive political atmosphere were fanned even more when Sarah Palin's political action committee targeted Democratic candidates who were running for office by using the Sarah Palin Political Action Committee's website to place a bull's eye target directly on the Democratic candidate as if the candidate was being seen through a rifle scope. I contend that behavior of this nature coupled with the venomous hate that Rush Limbaugh and Bill O'Rielly and others like them spew against minorities and minority sympathizers contributes to pushing mentally ill people like Jared Lee Loughner over the edge.

New York Times writer and Pulitzer Prize winner, Paul Krugman, wrote in an op-ed piece entitled; Climate of Hate, on January 9th, 2011, immediately after Jared Lee Loughner shot

Democratic congresswoman Gabrielle Gifford; "When you heard the terrible news from Arizona, were you completely surprised? Or were you, at some level, expecting something like this atrocity to happen? Put me in the latter category. I've had a sick feeling in the pit of my stomach ever since the final stages of the 2008 campaign. I remembered the upsurge in political hatred after Bill Clinton's election in 1992 — an upsurge that culminated in the Oklahoma City bombing. And you could see, just by watching the crowds at McCain-Palin rallies, that it was ready to happen again. The Department of Homeland Security reached the same conclusion: in April 2009 an internal report warned that right-wing extremism was on the rise, with a growing potential for violence. Conservatives denounced that report. But there has, in fact, been a rising tide of threats and vandalism aimed at elected officials, including both Judge John Roll, who was killed Saturday, and Representative Gabrielle Giffords. One of these days, someone was bound to take it to the next level. And now someone has. It's true that the shooter in Arizona appears to have been mentally troubled. But that doesn't mean that his act can or should be treated as an isolated event, having nothing to do with the national climate. and it's the saturation of our political discourse — and especially our airwaves — with eliminationist rhetoric that lies behind the rising tide of violence. Where's that toxic rhetoric coming from? Let's not make a false pretense of balance: it's coming, overwhelmingly, from the right. It's hard to imagine a Democratic member of Congress urging constituents to be "armed and dangerous" without being ostracized; but Representative Michele Bachmann, who did just that, is a rising star in the G.O.P."

President Barack Obama's State of the Union address on January 25th, 2011 skirted around the issue of race, prejudice and the frustrations of power addicted whites who are angry that the world is changing and moving forward without the permission of the traditional white male American power structure. President Obama also failed to directly verbalize the frustrations that African-Americans have living under the rule of white supremacy disguised as democratic capitalism, when it is obvious to all that the right wing's effort to limit access to education, job training and other boat lifting public policies are designed to trap the poor at the bottom of the economic ladder and insure that those at the top remain at the top. Those at the top are overwhelmingly white and male.

Obama has worked hard to be a reconciler but he has failed at being a type of socio- political surgeon like Dr. Martin Luther King, Jr. and South African President Nelson Mandela who vocally diagnosed the social patient as being infected with the cancerous tumors of racism, bigotry, prejudice and white supremacy. King and Mandela engaged the power structure in a type of psycho-social political surgery, using the surgical scalpel of Biblical truth, the idea of human dignity and equality for all, and transformative public policy to address the grievances of those who were adversely impacted by the white male power structure.

President Obama continues to apply band aids to the stab wounds of racial hatred and discrimination, he means well but he has missed a profound opportunity to help enlighten the White American masses that we do not live in a color blind society, that prejudice and racial hatred still exists and public policy is needed to address this issue directly. President Obama has failed to promote public policy that targets African-Americans by name and grievance; reparations may be a stretch, however all of the world can see how Black people in general and Black men in particular have been discriminated against and denied social, economic, and political opportunities based solely upon the color of our skin. Public policy in the form of jobs' bills, education grants, and guaranteed low interest business loans that directly benefit African-Americans would be a good start to right some of the centuries of wrongs experienced by Black people.

On December 19th, 2014 at the last Presidential press conference of the year, April Ryan, a journalist and White House correspondent for American Urban Radio, engaged President Obama with the following, read the transcript below;

President Obama: I'll ask -- April, go ahead.

April Ryan: Thank you, Mr. President. Last question, I guess. Six years ago this month, I asked you what was the state of black America in the Oval Office, and you said it was the "the best of times and the worst of times." You said it was the best of times in the sense that there was -- has never been more opportunity for African Americans to receive a good education, and the worst of times for unemployment and the lack of opportunity. We're ending 2014. What is the state of black America as we talk about those issues as well as racial issues in this country?

President Obama: "Like the rest of America, black America in the aggregate is better off now than it was when I came into office. The jobs that have been created, the people who've gotten health insurance, the housing equity that's been recovered, the 401 pensions that have been recovered -- a lot of those folks are African American. They're better off than they were. The gap between income and wealth of white and black America persists. And we've got more work to do on that front. I've been consistent in saying that this is a legacy of a troubled racial past of Jim Crow and slavery. That's not an excuse for black folks. And I think the overwhelming majority of black people understand it's not an excuse. They're working hard. They're out there hustling and trying to get an education, trying to send their kids to college. But they're starting behind, oftentimes, in the race. And what's true for all

Americans is we should be willing to provide people a hand up -- not a handout, but help folks get that good early childhood education, help them graduate from high school, help them afford college. If they do, they're going to be able to succeed, and that's going to be good for all of us."

Now that you have read what President Obama said, I want you to read it again, but this time I want you to listen to how President Obama goes to great lengths to avoid saying what needs to be done for BLACK PEOPLE specifically, he is always careful to group Black People as just Americans, when our social, economic, political and traumatized emotional condition is far different from the rest of American society.

President Obama: "Like the rest of America, black America in the aggregate is better off now than it was when I came into office."

LaGrone commentary: Mr. President we are not like the rest of America, the history of African-Americans is uniquely different from that of White America. Black America in the aggregate is not better off today than when you came into office. The poor are poorer and the black middle class is smaller today than six years ago.

President Obama: "The jobs that have been created, the people who've gotten health insurance, the housing equity that's been recovered, the 401 pensions that have been recovered -- a lot of those folks are African American. They're better off than they were. The gap between income and wealth of white and black America persists. And we've got more work to do on that front."

LaGrone commentary: According to the Center for Retirement Research at Boston College article written by Alicia H. Munnell and Christopher Sullivan entitled; 401(k) Plans and Race, November 2009, Number 9-24;

"The results from this exercise tell a goods news/bad news story. The good news is that 401(k) participation and contribution decisions do not appear to vary by race/ethnicity. That finding means that for comparably situated individuals, Blacks, Whites, and Hispanics respond in a similar fashion in terms of joining a 401(k) plan and deciding how much to contribute. The bad news is that Blacks, Whites, and Hispanics are not similarly situated. Blacks and Hispanics are less likely than Whites to be eligible for an employer-sponsored plan, less likely to have characteristics that would lead them to participate, and less likely to have the experience building wealth (as through homeownership) that would lead to high rates of contributions. So, the best way to boost retirement saving among minorities is not by thinking about race or ethnicity, but by focusing plan design and education efforts on those with lower levels of earnings and education."

This report tells us that African-Americans are not equally situated financially in the 401(k) market as White Americans are. Read the report in it's entirety and it is evident that African-Americans are not benefiting from the gains that Wall Street is making. Wall Street has recovered but Black Main Street is in shambles. I do not agree with the following that the reports says in the last sentence when the authors state; "So, the best way to boost retirement saving among minorities is not by thinking about race or ethnicity, but by focusing plan design and education efforts on those with lower levels of earnings and education." It seems that White Americans have a difficult time verbalizing the need for programs that specifically target African-Americans in a positive way. The report itself states that African-Americans are not fairing well with 401 (k) and wealth building, yet the authors come to the conclusion that plan design to solve the problem should target those with lower levels of earnings and education, most of whom are most likely African-American. Even when the data points to the need for specialized programs that to help African-Americans build wealth and get ahead in life, White America has a mental block, a psychological defense mechanism that prevents them from acknowledging that specific programs need to be developed that benefit African-Americans specifically. President Obama, more than most, should be keenly aware that programs that specifically benefit African-Americans are very much needed.

President Obama: "I've been consistent in saying that this is a legacy of a troubled racial past of Jim Crow and slavery. That's not an excuse for black folks. And I think the overwhelming majority of black people understand it's not an excuse."

LaGrone commentary: An Iraq War Veteran who may have become paralyzed during a bomb explosion does not have an excuse for not being able to walk, the paralyzed Veteran does not have an excuse for not being able to walk, but he has a reason as to why he can not walk. An EXCUSE and a REASON are two different things. Webster's Dictionary defines the word reason as 'a statement or fact that explains why something is the way it is, why someone does, think or say something or why someone behaves a certain way; a fact, condition, or situation that makes it proper or appropriate to do something or feel something. Webster's Dictionary defines the word excuse as 'to forgive someone for making a mistake, doing something wrong; to say that someone is not required to do something.

I am vigorously verbalizing that the biological, sociological, psychological and spiritual trauma and unfathomable abuses that generations of African-Americans have endured from chattel slavery, through segregationist Jim Crow Public Policy, present day prison industrial lynching, under-funded schools and predatory lending practices, just to name a few attacks that Black people experience, is not an excuse for why we are hurting so badly, these FACTS are solid, data driven, evidence based REASONS, as to why African-Americans are leading the country in so many negative health factors, economic factors, etc. We are intelligent enough to distinguish between an excuse and a reason. Wall Street made an excuse as to why the 2008 economic collapse occurred when in fact they are the CAUSE and REASON for that economic tragedy. President Obama consciously or sub-consciously finds himself lecturing Black people and in some instances 'talking down' to his own race as if we are ignorant in some way or other. At times President Obama sounds like the prototypical power addicted white male who is in denial about how his greed and self serving public policies adversely affect minority groups. President Obama's subconscious white male privilege thought process is even more evident in the next part of his statement below. Let's take a look at it.

President Obama: "They're working hard. They're out there hustling and trying to get an education, trying to send their kids to college. But they're starting behind, oftentimes, in the race. And what's true for all Americans is we should be willing to provide people a hand up -- not a handout, but help folks get that good early childhood education, help them graduate from high school, help them afford college. If they do, they're going to be able to succeed, and that's going to be good for all of us.

LaGrone Commentary: President Obama immediately turns to the catch phrases that make white people ears perk up and their head nod in agreement, whereas they believe that Black people just need to work harder and get a good education. President Obama makes it sound so damn simple, yet he conveniently turns a blind eye to the fact he is the President of the United States of America and the Republican Congress has treated him like he is a common street peddler or hustler. Cognitive reasoning will tell you that if power addicted white men treat PRESIDENT Obama in such a disrespectful way because he is a black man, then how much more disrespectful, hateful, and abusive are power addicted white males acting towards 'ordinary' black males throughout this country?

President Obama, if you know African-Americans are starting behind then where are the specific public policies that help all African-Americans get to the starting line with White Americans? I should not have to run faster just to catch up with White America! Why are Black people always asked to be super-human; run faster, jump higher, be twice as intelligent just in order to get a foot in the door? The demand from White America that I be a 'GREATER' Black Person in order to be considered 'EQUAL' to an 'AVERAGE' White Person is rooted in white supremacy ideology and it leads to emotional trauma and biological health issues for African-Americans. This racial induced trauma leads to excessive stress for African-Americans, and stress is the number one killer in the world!

CHAPTER TWELVE

2014 MIDTERM ELECTIONS: REPUBLICAN STRATEGY TO REMIND RED STATE WHITES TO HATE BARACK OBAMA

The 2014 midterm election results are a very telling sign of how traditionally conservative white people think. The National Republican Committee orchestrated a strategy that was guaranteed to stir up the racial fears and anti-black male sentiments that most of their electoral base carries. The National Republican Committee helped their Republican candidates to target campaign ads with messages that accused the Democratic political candidate of being merely a rubber stamp for President Obama, and this strategy worked like a charm. No Republican candidate offered any solutions for the nation's economic stagnation, educational decline, or any of the major issues that our nation is facing; they simply targeted the reptilian brain of their base electorate and reminded them to hate the black man Barack Obama.

The mainstream media acts as if they are dumfounded by the voting patterns of mostly poor working class whites who continue to vote for Republican candidates who openly profess to pass legislation that will suppress the minimum wage, export jobs, and limit educational opportunities for the poor and working poor. The mainstream media, mostly white commentators, can not brace their lips to just come out and say that these irrational voting patterns are reflective of mostly racist attitudes towards Barack Obama and any type of public policy that may remotely help people of color.

There is something sad and disturbing about these types of people, they feel that they are exercising their own free will when they cast their vote for the Republican candidate, but they are really being controlled by the white wealthy elite who uses them to push and promote an anti-black, anti-minority, anti- poor white, anti-working poor agenda. These poor white anti-Obama voters are cutting off their nose to spite their face.

When we analyze the types of political ads that caused these Republican candidates to get a bump in the polls and eventually get elected, we get a glimpse into the psychological mindset of these types of white conservative voters. Let's take a look at Iowa's Joni Ernst, the newly elected United States Senator from Iowa; she was behind in the polls until she ran a campaign ad that stated; "I grew up castrating hogs on an Iowa farm so when I get to Washington I will know how to cut pork. Washington is full of big spenders, let's make them squeal."

Joni Ernst is making a vow to go to

Washington, D.C., and inflict harm and violence upon President Obama's political agenda. Ernst intentionally provokes the sub-conscious in the white voters' superiority imagination, impressing the image of a black man having his genitals removed; invoking the image of a strong black man being cut down to size and being put back into his rightful subservient place beneath white people. Joni Ernst's reference to castration is reminiscent of how limp, lifeless black bodies would hang from the lynching tree, with the black male's genitals stuffed in the poor victim's mouth. Ernst's castration reference stirs up the power addicted white psyche memories of lynchings and how convenient it was just to take matters into their own hands when they felt that someone was hindering the white establishment social, economic and political agenda. There was no need for public debate, no engagement of critical problem solving thinking processes; no, the white mob would conclude that this Negro is causing us some type of perceived problem so let us just eliminate him or her, let us snuff out their life, let us erase them from the equation in order for us not to have to deal with the critical question that the Negro plight raises. These are the thought processes of those who assassinated Medgar Evers, Martin Luther King, Jr., John F. Kennedy, Robert Kennedy, and countless others.

In the state of North Carolina, Senator Kay Hagan was defeated by North Carolina General Assembly Speaker of the House, Republican Thom Tillis. Once again Tillis, like other Republican candidates, merely ran an anti-Obama campaign; Tillis used a campaign ad that stirred the subconscious racial fears of the white male voter by planting the subliminal message in the white male brain that Kay Hagan is a white woman who has a crush on Barack Obama. The Tillis ads drove home the message that Kay Hagan's voting record reflected that she voted with President Obama's political agenda 96% of the time. Tillis knows that most Democratic or Republican office holders do vote with their perspective political party the majority of the time, but Tillis and his campaign ad designers knew that this common sense fact would be displaced in the white male psyche because of the inference that Kay Hagan (white woman) is too close to Barack Obama (black man). The political ad that drove home this message consisted of a cute little white girl named Emily standing on stage in a spelling bee setting, the contest judges asked the little girl to spell HAGAN, the little girl asks for the definition of the word and a judge replies; "A Washington liberal from North Carolina who voted for the Obama agenda 96 percent of the time." The little girl then asks to hear the word HAGAN used in a sentence and another judge replies; "Kay Hagan was the deciding vote for Obama Care!" The little girl responds by spelling Hagan; "O.B.A.M.A.!" The spelling bee judges look at each other, nod their heads in approving unison and say; "Close enough!" The spelling bee judges agreed that spelling OBAMA is equivalent to spelling HAGAN!

White people like to think that most African-Americans voted for President Barack Obama for the mere reason that he is black, this is a sneaky way of saying that Black people do not have the intellectual capacity to engage in critical thinking and complex political strategy that leads them to vote for the best candidate that will promote their political interest. I contend that the race of a person is always one of the many factors that goes into any decision making process involving a person giving their vote of confidence to another person, however, white people are more notorious in voting for a candidate because he or she is white even though that candidate supports economic and educational policies that works against the interest of the poor white voter. I encourage you to find a demographic voting map online like CNN elections results 2014, take a look at the counties who voted majority republican in each State, and review the economic condition of those economically poor whites and compare their immediate needs to the long term anti-poor, anti-working class political agenda of the Republican party.

Black people showed more critical thinking skills and political self interest savvy when long time Mississippi Republican Senator, Thad Cochran, was in jeopardy of being ousted from the Senate seat he has held for over 35 years. African-Americans recognized that Thad Cochran's Tea Party opponent, Chris McDaniel, was extremely dangerous to the social, political, and educational interests of minorities, the poor and the working poor, therefore African-Americans took advantage of Mississippi's open primary system that was put into place to hinder black political candidates years ago. Forward thinking African-Americans were able to place their long term political interest above their emotional angst, cross party lines and vote for the Republican Thad Cochran during the open primary run-off election. The Black vote sent the Republican Senator Thad Cochran back to Washington, D.C.

Chris McDaniel's reaction to this savvy political strategy used by African-Americans to secure their political self-interest seemed to push Chris McDaniel into a state of rage, whereas he could hardly construct his sentences and communicate to the public during a press conference, it was like McDaniel was in shock that African-Americas had been so intelligent and savvy and willing to look beyond Thad Cochran's race and Republican Party affiliation and vote their own self-interest. Chris McDaniel even called the decisive votes cast for Thad Cochran by many Democratic leaning African-Americans as being 'tainted votes'. Is Chris McDaniel saying that these votes are smudged with tainted residue from the black hands that cast their ballot for Thad Cochran?

We are not living in a color blind society people, the power addicted white male does not feel comfortable talking about issues of race, social justice, or economic justice, yet he easily talks about the Taliban, ISIS, and other terrorist groups. He refuses to talk about the issue of race and prejudice because subconsciously the power addicted white male knows that he has been the terrorist that has haunted African-Americans for centuries. The power addicted white male has been Black America's Osama Bin Laden! The power addicted white male searches the world seeking out enemies and threats to the white male's way of life, but the power addicted white male refuses to take a long hard look in the mirror and deal with the power addicted enemy that lives within.

Lynching Barack Obama

Made in the USA
Charleston, SC
02 April 2015